Your Freedoms: The Bill of Rights

Over 150 years ago, the civil freedoms and liberties for the American people were set down in the Bill of Rights. While the fundamental concepts are unchanged, the complexities of our society have made for new and far-reaching interpretations.

Frank Kelly gives a lucid discussion of our first ten Amendments, beginning with a brief survey of how we won our rights. He then details each freedom, paints a picture of what America would be like without the Bill of Rights and concludes with a discussion of how we can keep our liberties.

YOUR FREEDOMS:
THE BILL OF RIGHTS

by FRANK K. KELLY

illustrated by Dirk Gringhuis

65-336

G. P. Putnam's Sons, New York

Second Impression

© 1964 by Frank K. Kelly

All Rights Reserved

Published simultaneously in the Dominion of
Canada by Longmans Canada Limited, Toronto

Library of Congress Catalog Card Number: 64-21587
12-16

Contents

CONTENTS

To J. R. Parten and
Louis Schweitzer
Directors of
The Fund for the Republic

Preface

THE MOST IMPORTANT subject before the American public during the last quarter century has been civil rights. At the same time, the least understood document has been the Bill of Rights, on which American civil rights are based. The Bill of Rights has been under steady, if covert, attack during this period by those who do not understand liberty and its guarantees.

Almost everyone is in favor of the phrase "Bill of Rights," yet large minorities, as shown by the polls, would favor forms of censorship, abridgment of free speech, wiretapping, and other invasions of privacy and personal freedom. The plain fact is that many Americans have never grasped the basic concepts on which American freedom is based—which are a profound respect for the individual, and a sense of certain inalienable rights and liberties which no person and no government can take away.

There are reasons why these concepts are not universally accepted. One reason is that civil liberty is based on a faith in man, on a belief that he comes to his fullest development in an atmosphere of freedom. There are people who do not have this faith in man, who think that a free man is more likely to get into trouble than become his noblest self. These people prefer the checks of authority to the encouragements of freedom. Mankind lived for centuries under authoritarian traditions; there are still men who prefer to be governed by others than to govern themselves.

Another reason for this lack of firm support of the Bill of Rights is that a lot of people don't know what it is. One high school student, when recently asked the meaning of the Bill of Rights, answered: "It means that a Negro kid can go to school in another school district if he wants to." No wonder this understanding is so limited; few learn much about the Bill of Rights in school, and good books on the subject are rare. There is a great need for lucid and thought-provoking dissertations on the Bill of Rights, written to start young people thinking about their rights and responsibilities, and it is to this need that Frank Kelly addresses himself.

Mr. Kelly, Vice-President of the Fund for the Republic, an organization founded to defend American civil liberties, and a prize-winning newspaper reporter, traces the history of each freedom guaranteed in the

Bill of Rights, recounting the conflicts that have arisen over each and the changing concepts of those freedoms over the years. He quotes from polls which show the lack of understanding of these fundamental American rights, and warns that we may lose them through ignorance or apathy. We may also lose them through fear—as we almost did in the early nineteen-fifties, when the late Senator Joseph McCarthy played on the anxieties of a war-weary public and sent a wave of fear and suspicion across the land.

What would happen if we lost our liberties? The author draws, in vivid detail, a picture of America without benefit of Bill of Rights, with young men kept in military service for indefinite periods; young people leaving school forced to take jobs assigned by the government; censorship of newspapers, books, radio and television programs; and people thrown into prison for speaking their minds. He concludes: "The very quality of American life would be gone. The independence, the willingness to speak out, which mark the true American everywhere, would be crushed. The eager exuberance, the lively restlessness, of Americans—noted by all foreign observers, cited by many as evidences of the creative atmosphere in America—would give way to cringing manners, fear of the police, fear of informers, fear of freedom itself."

The final question that Frank Kelly poses is: How can we keep our liberties? We must have an unshak-

11

able respect for other human beings, and that respect must be founded in a sense of human connection and brotherly love. We must have a large vision of the nature of man, and we must work toward fulfilling that nature. And we must understand the basic political philosophy underlying the Bill of Rights, which is "a perpetual search for the utmost meanings of life, a search conducted with full freedom of the mind and spirit."

Civil rights and civil liberties, though based on fundamental and unchanging concepts, constantly change and grow in their application. What will be the meaning of the Bill of Rights in the world that is emerging around us? The book quotes Justice William O. Douglas, who poses the problem of civil rights for the future: "The central problem of the age is the scientific revolution and all the wonder and damage it brings. . . . What are the Rights of Men against the machine as it becomes increasingly important? What Bill of Rights does man now need to keep a modicum of liberty? The forces allied against the individual have never been greater. The scientific revolution makes production and consumption the ends of society. Yet are they 'the pursuit of happiness'? The scientific revolution teaches conformity in a myriad of ways. The scientific revolution produces, indeed, a vast interdependendency among people. Where in this tightly knit regime is man to find liberty?"

PREFACE

To meet the challenges to liberty in the modern world, Americans must have a deep understanding of the nature of that liberty, a steadfast commitment to its guarantees, and a willingness to evolve new forms of its expression. This understanding and this commitment must begin young, must be part of the very texture of American life. Young people must experience it as part of the climate of growing up, and they must come to understand the meaning of that experience, through books such as these, for only then will it be truly part of them.

The American Bill of Rights is one of our most precious possessions; it can become one of our most precious gifts to the world. As Frank Kelly puts it, "The struggle in the world today between the forces of tyranny and the forces of freedom cuts across all national lines, all political parties, all divisions between East and West. It cannot be solved by war. . . . The problem of applying the American Bill of Rights to the people of all the states in the federal union of the United States may gradually become the problem of applying a Bill of Rights to all the people of the world."

ELMO ROPER

I How Your Rights Were Won

You take it for granted that you are an individual person. You have a name, an identity, a sense of being somebody different from everybody else. You have clothes, books, records, other possessions that belong to you. Looking at the world through your own eyes, you see things in a way that is different from the way other persons around you see things. You are a separate person.

As an individual, you have rights. In most of the countries in the world today, there are laws on the books guaranteeing the rights of individual human beings. Even in Communist countries, where the governments are extremely powerful, recognition is given in principle to the idea that every human being has certain basic rights that must be protected and respected.

In practice, of course, these rights are often impaired or violated by governments and other powerful organizations which claim control over their members. In totalitarian nations, the state comes first and the individual must be ready to sacrifice his rights whenever the sacrifice is demanded.

If you live in the United States, in western Europe, or in countries where the principle of individual freedom is strong, you have many liberties. You know that your ancestors suffered and fought for these liberties. You are not quite sure of your knowledge of how your rights were won. You may think that your liberties cannot be lost, because these freedoms were established nearly two centuries ago in America and the countries with many liberties have dominated the world in the twentieth century.

Actually the development of individual liberty came about through a slow process extending over thousands of years. Liberties have been won and lost, over and over again. In your time, you may lose your freedoms if you do not think about them and care about them.

The awakening of individual consciousness—the idea of every person as a separate person—grew slowly through the countless centuries of man's development. Primitive tribes generally considered men and women as parts of the tribes, not as free and separate beings.

In the countries around the Mediterranean Sea, a belief in the dignity of man as an individual gradually arose. The great thinkers and philosophers of China and the Far East had considered man as a river of humanity flowing into the enormous ocean of life in the universe. But the Greeks and the Jews considered man as an individual—as a single person, wondering where he had come from and where he was going.

In keeping with the Jewish tradition, Christianity asserted that every person was significant in the eyes of the Creator. Every human being had an eternal future. Every human being had been given an enormous gift of freedom by a God who was a personal God, a God interested in the fostering and full growth of every single person.

As the Christian culture spread, emperors as well as slaves accepted the idea that the essential worth of a man or woman did not depend upon his or her position in the material world. Even a slave had a soul, and that soul had a value beyond measure. Slaves were mis-

17

treated, slaves were compelled to live in poverty and servitude, yet every slave was a person and could not be regarded as a commodity like gold or iron.

The revolutionary ideas of Christianity led to the fall of the Roman Empire, the rise of new kingdoms, and finally to the spread of republics and democracies where the people were regarded as the sovereigns. The ideas of the Greek philosophers, which were close in many respects to the ideas of Christianity, helped to advance the cause of individual rights.

At the cost of many lives, men and women struggled through the ages to define and at last establish the list of rights to which they believed they were entitled. Many were punished with the whip and the rack, many were killed, many were sent into exile, but the cry for liberty could not be stifled.

These were the rights that came to be regarded as fundamental:

- The right to free speech, and with this was the right to be silent, not to be forced to testify or accuse one's self.
- The right to exercise freedom of belief and worship—this was closely associated with freedom of speech, and it came to mean that no one church should be given the endorsement or support of the government.
- The right to assemble, to discuss grievances, and to seek changes in government or society.

• The right to protection of life and property against seizure by rulers.

• The right to a fair trial by a "jury of peers"—that is, by a group of persons of the same standing.

• The right to be protected against cruel and unusual punishments—outlawing physical tortures such as burning, blinding, and mutilation of limbs.

• The right to have independent counsel when facing charges brought against an individual by rulers.

These ideas flourished in all the countries affected by the Judeo-Christian scriptures and the philosophy of the individualistic Greeks. In three Western countries—England, France, and Germany—the ideas finally sparked a series of rebellions against princes and nobles. The demand for individual freedom led to bloody fighting, the beheading of kings, the slaughter of thousands in fierce combat.

In England there arose a movement called Puritanism. It was composed of people who left the Church of England because they felt that church had not been sufficiently purified from corrupt practices. Dissenters in religion and in politics, some of the Puritans were driven from England. Some of them fled to Holland and then went to North America, where they founded colonies on the shores of Massachusetts Bay.

These Puritan colonists felt that the rights of Englishmen, won in earlier generations, were being destroyed in England by monarchs who despised Parliament or would not call the Parliament into session. In the twenty years between 1620 and 1640, the Puritans transferred more than 25,000 selected men and women to what became known as New England. In 1640, after Parliament had again assembled in old England, many of the Puritan colonists returned to the motherland. But those who remained in Massachusetts and other colonies developed ideas of independence which later flamed in the American Revolution.

During the period of colonial settlement, Catholic immigrants under the leadership of Lord Calvert formed a community in Maryland with an atmosphere of freedom. Under Calvert's charter, a representative assembly was established. This body, like the House of Burgesses in the neighboring colony of Virginia, soon asserted its rights to pass legislation for all free men within its area.

In Colonial Virginia, the settlers claimed the rights and privileges of Englishmen—which included free speech and the right to a jury trial. The House of Burgesses, as the assembly was called, declared in 1624 that it had the right to control taxation in the colony.

Harsh and intolerant as they were in some ways, the Puritans in New England cleared the way for the growth of American ideas of individual freedoms. The pioneers in Maryland and Virginia, in Rhode Island

and other colonies also made it clear to their governors that they felt entitled to the rights assured to every freeholder in England under "the common law."

Every free man in England claimed that the sovereign ruler had a responsibility to protect his life, his liberty, and his property from arbitrary assaults. These rights were traced back to the twelfth century. The use of juries was first mentioned in 1166, in connection with a criminal case, although there are some records indicating that juries were used a century earlier in civil cases.

It was in the twelfth century, however, according to historians, that the right of accused persons to have "learned counsel" was recognized. Statutes in 1275 and 1444 were aimed at prohibiting excessive fines and excessive bail bonds. Sheriffs were ordered to give prisoners every opportunity to be released on bail unless their crimes were very serious.

During the 150 years which followed the landings in Massachusetts, Virginia, Maryland and other colonies, the settlers in the new land had to keep up a constant struggle against attempts by the English kings and royal governors to bring them under absolute control. In Virginia, an influx of royalists overthrew the colonial democracy of the early days and power shifted into the hands of the governor and his council. In New England, royal governors fought to control the rising tide of popular democratic government.

When James II came to the throne of England late in the seventeenth century, he consolidated all of New England into one province and appointed Sir Edmund Andros as governor-general. Andros was already in control of New York and New Jersey; these colonies were brought into the New England province. King James took out of the new charter all provisions for popular representation, and Andros had the powers of a dictator.

After the English revolution of 1688, the colonists regained their old forms of government. Under bold leaders, the people of Boston and neighboring towns took Andros a prisoner and captured the royal fort in Boston harbor. A new charter was granted to Massachusetts in 1691.

The revolution of 1688 in England foreshadowed in some ways the American revolt which came nearly a century later. James II lost his throne because he violated the rights that Englishmen were determined to maintain. In 1689 the Parliament adopted a declaration of rights and liberties, asserting that it was illegal for a king to suspend laws without Parliament's consent or to levy taxes without Parliament's approval.

Indicating the principles that were to be embodied in the American Bill of Rights, the Declaration of 1689 said that British subjects had the right to petition the king freely, that freedom of speech and debate in Parliament could not be questioned, and that the raising or keeping of a standing army in a time of peace without the consent of Parliament was not legal. The Declaration specified that elections of members of Parliament should be freely held, and Parliament should be frequently convened.

In this Declaration, Parliament said that excessive bail should not be required of any person accused of a crime, excessive fines were not permitted, and cruel and unusual punishments were prohibited. A person under a criminal charge was guaranteed a trial by "impartial jurors," and fines and forfeitures of accused persons before conviction were not lawful.

Many historians rank the Declaration of 1689 with the Magna Carta as the most important statements of rights and liberties in English annals. The Magna Carta, signed by King John at Runnymede in 1215, secured the rights of barons and nobles, whereas the statement of 1689 provided for the rights and liberties of a great many Englishmen. Before William and Mary took over the royal powers in England (after the fall of James II), they had to acknowledge the validity of the Declaration.

The colonists in New England, Maryland, Virginia and other areas in America were certain that the statement of 1689 applied to them as well as to residents of England. Chief Justice Holt of the highest court in England affirmed their position when he ruled in 1694 that the rights of Englishmen extended to those in the colonies. "All the laws in force in England are in force there," Justice Holt said. And twenty-six years later, in 1720, Attorney General West gave an opinion that the common law of England was the law in the colonies unless there was "some private Act to the contrary."

When King George III came along in the 1760's and undertook to force the American colonies to pay increased taxes without giving the colonists the right to be represented in Parliament, an explosive situation developed. "No taxation without representation" became a battle cry, and by 1775 the colonies were in a state of rebellion.

In 1776, American leaders took the drastic step of asserting their independence. Saying that they spoke for the people of "the United States of America," these leaders appealed to the world for support against the British king, vividly describing their grievances against him. In effect, they found George III and his ministers guilty of un-British activities: the king and his councilors had failed to apply the Declaration of 1689 to free men in the colonies.

The tremendous sentences in the Declaration of American Independence rang forth for all mankind to hear: "When, in the course of human events, it becomes necessary for one people to dissolve the political bands which have connected them with one another, and to assume, among the powers of the earth, the separate and equal station to which the laws of nature and of nature's God entitled them, a decent respect to the opinions of mankind requires that they should declare the causes which impel them to the separation.

"We hold these truths to be self-evident—that all men are created equal; that they are endowed by their Creator with certain inalienable rights; that among these are life, liberty, and the pursuit of happiness. That, to secure these rights, governments are instituted among men, deriving their just powers from the consent of the governed. . . ."

The men who signed that Declaration of 1776 knew they were risking their lives, their fortunes, and their honor. But they were prepared to take the risks. Behind them stood long lines of ancestors who had risked all for liberty in other centuries.

"Whenever any form of government becomes destructive of these ends, it is the right of the people to alter or to abolish it, and to institute a new government, laying its foundation on such principles, and organizing its powers in such form, as to them shall seem most likely to effect their safety and happiness," the American Declaration said.

Those were bold words in the eighteenth century, when the earth was dominated by the might of kings. Those are still bold words today, when many people shiver at the revolutions occurring in Asia, Africa, and Latin America. The men who founded the United States knew what they were doing, and they knew it was an awesome thing. They proclaimed "the right of the people to alter or to abolish" any form of government.

The signers of the Declaration were not a bearded rabble of anarchists or bomb throwers. They were sober, solid, substantial gentlemen. Many of them had sizable estates. Some of them thought they might be hanged for what they were doing.

But they went ahead, because they were moved by the spirit of liberty. And the spirit of liberty has prevailed in the nation they founded. In spite of fits of fear and in spite of the dire predictions of those who distrust the people, the nation has survived and grown under God to a towering height of prosperity and power.

The Declaration of Independence, the Constitution, and the Bill of Rights—these are the sacred documents of America. These are statements revered and respected wherever freedom thrives.

Let us now consider the Bill of Rights, the charter of our fundamental liberties.

II The American Revolution and Our Charter of Liberties

THE American Revolution was fought and won by a loose organization of states—the thirteen colonies, linked together by the Articles of Confederation which were ratified between 1778 and 1781 while George Washington's army was carrying on the struggle against the British. Without the aid supplied by France and other allies, it is doubtful whether Washington's forces could have triumphed. The Continental Congress lacked the power to raise taxes, and without tax revenues the soldiers could not be paid regularly and the rapid depreciation in the value of the United States dollar could not be controlled. The states ignored many of the resolutions passed by the Congress, participated in tax and trade "wars" among themselves, and conditions were finally so chaotic that foreign diplomats wondered whether the United States should be regarded as one nation or thirteen.

Alarmed by the rebellion led by Captain Daniel Shays in 1786, the inflation of the currency and other signs of approaching anarchy, a convention of businessmen gathered in Annapolis that year and suggested that Congress call an assembly of citizens to revise the Articles of Confederation. Congress acted on the suggestion, and a Federal Convention met in 1787 to see what could be done. The delegates were not authorized to draw up a new constitution, but decided to do so under the leadership of Washington, Benjamin Franklin, James Madison, George Mason, Oliver Ellsworth and other men of property and power. Thomas Jefferson and John Adams were overseas on special missions, and did not take part; but both believed that the establishment of a stronger federal government was necessary.

28

The Constitution of 1787 is the one under which we are living today. It has lasted longer than any other written constitution drawn up by the leaders of any other major nation. It has been hailed for many years as a masterpiece of political wisdom.

Yet it was subjected to strife when it was submitted to the original thirteen states for ratification. In several important states, only a few more votes were cast for the Constitution than were cast against it. Some historians have contended that it would have been defeated if it had been placed before the people in a referendum. As it was, approval was given by state legislatures after stormy debates.

The attacks on the Constitution came principally from two sources—from those who felt that it weakened the states too much, and from those who wanted a Bill of Rights. Jefferson, the author of the Declaration of Independence, was one of the leaders who felt that a charter of personal rights and protections for the states had to be added to the basic document as quickly as possible.

In the First Congress that assembled after the Constitution had been adopted, Madison proposed a series of twelve amendments. The First Amendment as we have it today was actually the third one on Madison's list; his first two amendments dealt with the number of Representatives to be elected and with the compensation to be paid to members of Congress. He wrote his Bill of Rights on the basis of proposals offered by a number of state legislators during the conflict over the Constitution.

Many of the states had already developed Bills of Rights. The most notable was the Virginia Declaration of Rights, which was largely composed by a wealthy planter, George Mason. Its first section placed property rights high among the "inherent rights" with which men were endowed "by nature." This section declared: "All men are by nature equally free and independent and have certain inherent rights, of which, when they enter into a state of society, they cannot by any compact deprive or divest their posterity; namely, the enjoyment of life and liberty, with the means of acquiring and possessing property, and pursuing and obtaining happiness and safety."

Life, liberty and the pursuit of happiness were generally accepted as among the fundamental rights of man. Madison and the others who pushed the federal Bill of Rights through the First Congress, acting under the Constitution, evidently felt that property rights were adequately protected by the Constitution and by the American tradition of regarding the possession of private property as an essential element in man's happiness. The Americans had moved a long way from the closely regulated economic system which had prevailed in England, and were determined to preserve the individual's free access to property.

The provisions of the Bill of Rights were affected by the debate in Congress and by the views expressed to Madison by Thomas Jefferson in letters from Paris. Jefferson declared: "A bill of rights is what the people are entitled to against every government on earth, general or particular; and what no just government should refuse or rest on inference." He asked for plain words "providing clearly, and without the aid of sophism, for freedom of religion, freedom of the press, protection against standing armies, restriction of monopolies, the eternal and unremitting force of the habeas corpus laws, and trials by jury in all matters of fact triable by the laws of the land, and not by the laws of nations."

Jefferson was impatient with the ideas of James Wilson, a Pennsylvania lawyer who had taken part in the Constitutional Convention of 1787, and felt that a charter of rights and liberties was not necessary. Wilson claimed that the framers of the Constitution had reserved many rights to the people. The Constitution did not say that any branch of the federal government had power to take away freedom of religion, of the press, or any of the liberties Jefferson was so eager to preserve. So Mr. Wilson thought that Mr. Jefferson had no cause for alarm.

"I consider all the ill as established which may be established," Jefferson told Madison in a strongly phrased letter. "I have a right to nothing which another has a right to take away; and Congress will have a right to take away trials by jury in all civil cases." And Jefferson said again that he wanted a federal Bill of Rights "to guard liberty against the legislative as well as the executive branches of the government."

Alexander Hamilton, one of the most ardent defenders of the Constitution, saw no need for the inclusion of a charter of liberties in the document, and gave his reasons eloquently in No. 84 of *The Federalist* papers, one of the statements issued by those who advocated its ratification.

"Bills of rights are, in their origin, stipulations between kings and their subjects," Hamilton wrote. "Such was Magna Charta, obtained by the barons, sword in hand, from King John. Such were the subsequent confirmations of that charter by succeeding princes. Such was the Petition of Right assented to by Charles I in the beginning of his reign. Such, also, was the Declaration of Right presented by the Lords and Commons to the Prince of Orange in 1688, and afterwards thrown into the form of an act of parliament called the Bill of Rights.

"It is evident, therefore, that according to their primitive signification, they have no application to constitutions, professedly founded upon the power of the people, and executed by their immediate representatives and servants. Here, in strictness, the people surrender nothing; and as they retain every thing they have no need of particular reservations."

Hamilton pointed out that the preamble to the Constitution proclaimed: "We, the people of the United States, in order to . . . secure the blessings of liberty to ourselves and our posterity, do ordain and establish this Constitution for the United States of America." Nothing could be clearer than that, Hamilton believed.

"Here is a better recognition of popular rights, than volumes of those aphorisms which make the principal figure in several of our State bills of rights, and which would sound much better in a treatise on ethics than in a constitution of government," Hamilton continued.

"I go further, and affirm that bills of rights, in the sense and to the extent in which they are contended for, are not only unnecessary . . . but would even be dangerous. They would contain various exceptions to powers not granted; and, on this very account, would afford a colorable pretext to claim more than were granted.

"For why declare that things shall not be done which there is no power to do? Why, for instance, should it be said that the liberty of the press shall not be restrained, when no power is given by which restrictions may be imposed? I will not contend that such a provision would confer a regulating power; but it is evident that it would furnish, to men disposed to usurp, a plausible pretence for claiming that power. They might urge with a semblance of reason, that the Constitution ought not to be charged with the absurdity of providing against the abuse of an authority which was not given, and that the provision against restraining the liberty of the press afforded a clear implication, that a power to prescribe proper regulations concerning it was intended to be vested in the national government. This may serve as a specimen of the numerous handles which would be given to the doctrine of constructive powers, by the indulgence of an injudicious zeal for bills of rights."

Hamilton insisted that the liberty of the press, as well as other freedoms, must altogether depend upon the support of public opinion and "on the general spirit of the people and of the government." He wrote: "Here, after all, must we seek for the only solid basis of all our rights.

"The truth is . . . that the Constitution is itself, in every rational sense, and to every rational purpose, a bill of rights," Hamilton concluded. "Is it one object of a bill of rights to declare and specify the political privileges of the citizens in the structure and administration of the government? This is done in the most ample and precise manner. . . . Is another object of a bill of rights to define certain immunities and modes of proceeding, which are relative to personal and private concerns? This . . . has also been attended to, in a variety of cases, in the same plan."

In one sense, Hamilton was certainly right. The Constitution had been written by men who were determined to form a government with limited powers, controlled by the people. (The people, in their minds, were persons of education and substance, capable of considering the problems of government rationally and rather objectively.)

But Thomas Jefferson raised the great questions. In one of his articles, Jefferson said: "Is the spirit of the people an infallible, a permanent reliance? Is it government? Is this the kind of protection we receive in return for the rights we give up? Besides, the spirit of the times may alter, will alter. Our rulers will become corrupt, our people careless. A single zealot may commence persecution, and better men be his victims. It can never be too often repeated that the time for fixing every essential right on a legal basis is while our rulers are honest and ourselves united."

Jefferson foresaw that the high and noble enthusiasm of the revolution would not last. He was aware of the fact that the generation which had achieved so much was a rare generation. He wanted that generation to place upon the scrolls of the nation a clear and simple statement of fundamental rights, so that Congressmen and Presidents and judges of the coming generations would have stated before their eyes a list of the liberties regarded as fundamental by the Founding Fathers of the American nation.

He was afraid that the people would be forgotten and their rights might be disregarded. In an article on the administration of justice, he wrote: "They will forget themselves, but in the sole faculty of making money, and will never think of uniting to effect a due respect for their rights." He rallied the forces for a federal Bill of Rights, and his friends and followers entered the fray with passion and persistence.

Jefferson, Madison and other advocates of a written Bill of Rights triumphed. Hamilton, Wilson and others who honestly contended that the very spirit of the Constitution was the spirit of liberty were acknowledged to have much in favor of their arguments, but most of the people who could vote one way or another decided that the basic freedoms should be spelled out in unmistakable terms.

Deep questions related to man's nature and the working of human society were at issue in these struggles. Was freedom a matter of the spirit or did it have to be established, identified and protected by the law? Was it a good thing to depend upon public opinion for final sanctions of what could and could not be permitted? Or were there some "inalienable rights," beyond the power of the people to give or to take away?

In the eighteenth century, many men believed in a "natural law." Men felt that there were certain principles of human life which had been laid down by the Creator of the universe. These principles were above human governments, and men could appeal to them with the expectation that their rational fellows would pay heed to those principles.

Many of the men who shaped the American Revolution and fought for the Bill of Rights believed that John Locke, the English philosopher, was correct when he asserted that "to understand political power aright, and derive it from its original, we must consider what state all men are naturally in—and that is a state of perfect freedom to order their actions and dispose of their persons and possessions as they think fit, within the bounds of the law of nature, without asking leave, or depending upon the will of any other man. . . ." They also thought Locke was right when he added: "But though this be a state of liberty, yet it is not a state of license. . . . The state of nature has a law of nature to govern it, which obliges everyone; and reason, which is that law, teaches all mankind who will but consult it, that, being all equal and independent, no one ought to harm another in his life, health, liberty, or possessions."

Governments were created to preserve those principles, the American leaders believed. The "positive law," which could be derived from the "law of nature," could be expressed in constitutions and in bills of rights. So the basic liberties of the individual, although not given by the government, could be defined and protected in charters supported by the people acting through the government.

In the minds of the men who framed the Constitution and the Bill of Rights, liberty and law were linked. Rules of fair conduct, prescribing the procedures to be followed by Congress, the President and the courts, were bulwarks of liberty. To maintain freedom, men had to make sure that the power of the government was positively on the side of freedom, not simply enforcing negative prohibitions.

The government established by the United States was a new kind of government—it was to be limited, it was to be a servant of the citizens, and it was to do its utmost to encourage all generations of Americans to secure the blessings of liberty for themselves and all those coming along in the stream of history.

III The First Amendment:
Freedom of Religion

To SPEAK FREELY, to attend meetings, to circulate petitions, to go to church or to stay home, to criticize our governors and our courts and our legislators —we take these things as a matter of course in modern America. All of these activities are given constitutional protection by the first article of the ten articles which form the Bill of Rights, and this article keeps the heart of a free society alive and throbbing. It covers all of the fundamental functions we must exercise in order to be free and to stay free.

In bold, sharp words the Amendment begins with this ringing commandment: *"Congress shall make no law. . . ."* Before we go on to consider what Congress was forbidden to touch, let us think about the audacity of those words. In the Constitution, Congress had been established as the legislative organ of the people—with power to raise taxes, to form military forces, to declare war on other nations. And here was an Amendment starting out by saying that there were certain laws Congress could not pass.

There was no time limit in those words. Looking ahead into the foreseeable future, the authors of Article I simply said: *"Congress shall make no law. . . ."* As plainly as they could, they indicated to the world that there were certain areas of human freedom which were not to be limited by legislative action, in the present or in the future.

Here are the areas, specifically outlined in the full text of the amendment: "Congress shall make no law respecting an establishment of religion, or prohibiting the free exercise thereof; or abridging the freedom of speech or of the press; or the right of the people peaceably to assemble, and to petition the government for a redress of grievances." No one has yet devised a clearer or better statement of the indispensable rights of real citizens.

Let us restate these rights and look at them separately. The right to worship God in one's own way, without danger of being condemned or tortured or burned at the stake for differing from the beliefs of the authorities, was lifted before the eyes of all men as a right to be upheld for all time. Our ancestors had learned from bitter experiences that the power of the government should not be placed behind any religious body: the temptation to use force to compel adherence to a creed became too great, and persecutions occurred.

The value of religion, its importance in the nation's life and in the lives of citizens, was fully recognized in the Amendment. Later generations interpreted the religion clause to mean that Congress could encourage various forms of religion, but was not to interfere with any religious practices—except in extreme cases, such as the practice of polygamy.

Despite the clarity of the First Amendment, the relationships between the churches and the government in the United States have been complex and confused, especially in recent years. Judges, cabinet members, school administrators, army officers, Congressmen and Presidents have tried to resolve the difficulties in conflicting ways.

The Amendment certainly meant that Congress

could not set up an official church for Americans and could not use legislative power to prevent various sects from arising. It did not say, however, that Congress could not aid religion in general. And Congress has done so—by granting tax exemption to religious groups, by providing pay for chaplains in the armed forces, by making federal funds available for books, hot lunches and other services to children in religious schools. The so-called "wall of separation between Church and State" has been ignored or pierced in many places.

Questions of religious freedom have come before the Supreme Court of the United States in a number of crucial cases. Whether the Founding Fathers intended it to be so or not, the Court has been the arbiter of the "constitutionality" of federal laws for more than 160 years, and has insisted in recent decades that state legislatures cannot lawfully enact bills that violate the fundamental clauses of the First Amendment. The Court's right to strike down legislation has been challenged again and again, but it has not yet been removed from its role as the high umpire in the American system.

The clear and simple words of the Amendment have not seemed so clear and simple under changing conditions. Faced by complex cases, the Supreme Court justices have had to decide for themselves what "religion" means, and what "an establishment of religion" might be.

Examples of such cases give indications of what complexities can be involved. The judges have had to rule on whether it is lawful to make children of certain sects salute the United States flag when the religious beliefs of the children forbid such compulsory salutes; whether a state could use tax funds to pay the bus fares of parochial school pupils; whether New York schools could ask students to recite a prayer; and other cases in which opinions differed strongly. Being men of varied backgrounds and philosophies, the justices have not been consistent in their rulings.

Yet their decisions, while swinging occasionally from one position to another, have largely defined the meanings of the Bill of Rights and particularly the meanings of the First Amendment. Let us take a look at their opinions in a few significant decisions.

In the flag-salute case, the Court sustained the right of Jehovah's Witnesses to refrain from participating in a ceremony honoring the flag. Instead of saluting, members of the Witnesses sect offered to give the following declaration: "I have pledged my unqualified allegiance and devotion to Jehovah, the Almighty God, and to His Kingdom, for which Jesus commands all Christians to pray. I respect the flag of the United States as a symbol of freedom and justice to all. I pledge allegiance and obedience to all the laws of the United States that are consistent with God's law, as set forth in the Bible."

When he announced the Court's decision in this case on June 14, 1943, Justice Robert H. Jackson gave a statement which has been quoted frequently in the succeeding years. It has become accepted as a beautiful summation of the principles that give continuing life to the Bill of Rights.

"We set up government by consent of the governed," Justice Jackson said. "The Bill of Rights denies those in power any legal opportunity to coerce that consent. Authority here is to be controlled by public opinion, not public opinion by authority.

"The case is made difficult not because the principles of its decision are obscure but because the flag involved is our own. Nevertheless, we apply the limitations of the Constitution with no fear that freedom to be intellectually and spiritually diverse or even contrary will disintegrate the social organization.

"To believe that patriotism will not flourish if patriotic ceremonies are voluntary and spontaneous instead of a compulsory routine is to make an unflattering estimate of the appeal of our institutions to free minds.

"We can have intellectual individualism and the rich cultural diversities that we owe to exceptional minds only at the price of occasional eccentricity and abnormal attitudes. When they are so harmless to others or to the state as those we deal with here, the price is not too great. But freedom to differ is not

44

limited to things that do not matter much. That would be a mere shadow of freedom. The test of its substance is the right to differ as to things that touch the heart of the existing order.

"If there is any fixed star in our constitutional constellation, it is that no official, high or petty, can prescribe what shall be orthodox in politics, nationalism, religion, or other matters of opinion, or force citizens to confess by word or act their faith therein. If there are any circumstances which permit an exception, they do not now occur to us."

Six of the nine justices approved the decision rendered by Justice Jackson. Justice Felix Frankfurter spoke for the minority of dissenters in his opinion: "Of course patriotism cannot be enforced by the flag salute. But neither can the liberal spirit be enforced by judicial invalidation of illiberal legislation. Our constant preoccupation with the constitutionality of legislation rather than with its wisdom tends to preoccupation of the American mind with a false value."

Most of the Protestant sects, the Roman Catholic Church, the members of Jewish temples and synagogues, have generally regarded the obligations of citizenship—such as flag ceremonies and military service—as acceptable in the light of their religious ideas. Whether such obligations are regarded as legally enforceable or not, members of these religious groups have accepted them. Quakers, Seventh-day Adventists and Jehovah's Witnesses, however, have regarded the bearing of arms even for national defense as contrary to their precepts.

Our courts have generally held that the religious freedom clause of the First Amendment cannot be invoked to exempt conscientious objectors from military duty. In two World Wars, however, the Congress of the United States has given some recognition to the idea that religious beliefs or conscientious convictions might prevent some citizens from using arms.

Under the 1941 draft law, persons conscientiously opposed to participation in war (if their objections were found to be validly based on their beliefs and practices) could be placed in noncombatant units. Some conscientious objectors served heroically as ambulance drivers and as medical aides on the field of battle. Others were assigned to civilian work camps under military control.

In the 1948 selective service legislation, persons who could prove that their religious ideas would not allow them to serve in the armed forces were given deferments. Atheistic pacifists were not included, however. Only persons who acknowledged a Supreme Being could qualify for deferment. Three years later, the law was amended to require two years of national service by conscientious objectors in an acceptable government or nonprofit agency.

The attitudes of religious groups toward the federal

government and state government have been much affected by the history of their relations with governments. The Protestant groups, long dominant in American society, have been divided among themselves and have taken varying positions at different periods in American history and in different parts of the country. Protestants in the South have opposed aid to parochial schools but have insisted that Christian practices in public schools were not in violation of the First Amendment.

Some Protestant clergymen have strongly advocated an absolute separation of church and state because they believe that the church must be completely free to be a critic and conscience for human society. In such matters as tax exemptions for religious agencies, these clergymen feel that such exemptions should be opposed because the church must regard any special status in economics or politics as an obstacle to the fulfillment of its role as a body above and beyond the temporal world.

The Roman Catholic Church has flourished in the United States, and Catholic leaders generally have found themselves able to work in harmony with state and federal governments. In an authoritative book entitled *We Hold These Truths*, the Rev. John Courtney Murray, S.J., a noted Catholic theologian, recently stated that the provisions of the First Amendment could be described as "articles of peace." He said they had enabled Americans of various faiths to work out their controversies by peaceful means.

John Cogley, Catholic layman and columnist for *The Commonweal,* declared in an article published in *Ave Maria,* a Catholic monthly:

"Freedom of religion, in the American scheme, is regarded as something to be encouraged. The amendment separating church and state was not written to discourage men from being religious, to keep society from acting in conformity with its religious heritage, or to prevent the citizenry from realizing the consequences of its religious commitments in the workaday world. The restrictions on the activities of the state in the realm of the church, and of the church in the realm of the state, were made in order to keep some men, both religious and irreligious, from interfering with the right of their neighbors to believe and behave as conscience directed.

"Seen this way, religious liberty is a *distinct* civil liberty. It is related to freedom of thought, freedom of speech, and freedom of association, but it is not subsumed by them. It is freedom *for* religion. The liberty of the unreligious or the anti-religious, freedom *from* religion, is taken care of in the same Constitution by the provisions for freedom of speech and assembly, and the general American respect for freedom of conscience."

The approaches of Catholics, Protestants and Jews

to the religion clause of the First Amendment were thoughtfully examined by Rabbi Arthur Hertzberg, lecturer in history at Columbia University, in an article in the April, 1963, issue of *Commentary,* a publication of the American Jewish Committee. Rabbi Hertzberg declared that while there were deep differences within the Jewish community "the overwhelming weight of both feeling and opinion among contemporary Jews is for the strictest kind of separation between religion and the state—and even between religion and society."

"Nor is this opinion merely a tactical response to the current situation in America," Rabbi Hertzberg wrote. "It is in fact the expression of an attitude to society that has deep roots in Jewish history, especially in the Western experience of the last eighteen centuries."

Jewish leaders in America, struggling to maintain their independence and their religious traditions in a society largely controlled by Christian or secular culture, have tried to get the Supreme Court to view the Amendment as establishing a complete line of distinction between the areas reserved for religion and the areas reserved for the state. Nonreligious leaders, differing from the Christian and Jewish positions, have contended that the religion clause guarantees freedom for nonbelievers as well as believers.

Advocates of all viewpoints, however, are in strong agreement on one thing—the First Amendment is at the heart of our conceptions of fundamental freedoms. No one with any substantial following advocates modification or repeal of the Amendment.

Americans of many backgrounds have consistently supported Justice Jackson's statement that "no official, high or petty, can prescribe what shall be orthodox in politics, nationalism, religion, or other matters of opinion." If Americans of coming generations hold to that position, freedom of religion will be secure in the future.

IV The First Amendment:
Freedom of Speech and
of the Press

IF YOU HAVE ever spent any time in a country ruled by a dictator—as this writer has—you know what the choking sense of censorship is, the feeling of a fierce hand at your throat, cutting off your speech. In Venezuela, some years ago, the dictator was an army colonel whose initials were P.J. Entering a restaurant in Caracas with a friend, the writer was told: "Be careful about what you say here. P.J.'s men will be listening." The question came: "What will happen if I'm not careful?" The answer was swift: "If you're lucky, you'll be kicked out of the country on the next plane. If you're not lucky, nobody will see you again." Fear was in the air—a thick and poisonous fog of fear.

Thanks to the determination of our ancestors and to the devotion of the generations preceding us, we have free speech in the United States. We can say that a Congressman is stupid, that a judge is corrupt, that a President is doing a poor job, that a governor is fumbling and incompetent—and we know that we will not be taken off to jail or shot for saying what we think. Let us pray that this freedom will always be cherished and defended.

Whatever else he may be, a man is a talking animal, a being who finds his own significance in communicating with the men and women around him. A man who talks to himself alone is unbalanced, not participating in the full life of humanity. A man who is afraid to talk has a noose around his neck and a sickening gag in his mouth.

Yet freedom of speech is a dangerous thing. Everyone knows that. A man may incite a mob to start a riot, or to lynch another man because that man has black skin. A man or a woman may scream "Fire!" in a crowded hall, causing a panic that may bring death or injuries to others. Tormented, hate-ridden people may spread lies about their neighbors, slandering reputations, arousing rage against Jews or Negroes or Catholics or anyone whose ways are not their ways.

How far should freedom of speech be allowed to go?

No one knows the answer to this question. Judges and lawyers have wrestled with it for centuries. College trustees, confronted by cantankerous professors voicing unpopular opinions, have had to suffer the stings of criticism for defending "full academic freedom of expression."

In theory, everybody is in favor of free speech. In practice, nearly everybody draws a line at one point or another. Parents limit what they say in front of their children. Doctors are cautious about what they talk about in the presence of their patients. Teachers who know that students may report their opinions to parents sometimes censor themselves.

Complete freedom of speech has not existed in any nation. The United States has come close to it, perhaps closer than any other large country, but in the U.S.A. there have been limitations and there are still limitations on this freedom. You can't indulge in slander or libel with impunity. You can't promote subversive activities or draft dodging without running a serious risk of fines or imprisonment.

But the First Amendment states, bluntly and baldly,

that Congress shall not abridge the freedom of speech or of the press. How are the limitations reconciled with the clear statement of the Amendment?

There have been a few judges—in our time, principally Supreme Court Justice Black—who have held that freedom of speech is an absolute right which cannot be hedged or limited by judicial rulings. Generally, however, the courts have come to accept the idea that freedom of speech is a social right rather than an individual right. According to this view, freedom of speech should be protected as far as possible because society needs to hear the expression of every possible idea, but in times of crisis a society has the power to curtail or even suppress certain ideas.

Thomas Jefferson, consistently, was in favor of a maximum degree of free speech. In a letter to James Madison in January, 1787, he wrote: "Societies exist under three forms, sufficiently distinguishable. 1. Without government, as among our Indians. 2. Under governments, wherein the will of everyone has a just influence, as is the case in England, to a slight degree, and in our states, in a great one. 3. Under governments of force, as is the case in all other monarchies and most other republics. To have an idea of the curse of existence under these last, they must be seen. It is a government of wolves over sheep."

To give the will of everyone a chance to exert "a just influence," Jefferson felt that free speech had to be enshrined and zealously defended. He thought that the noblest of men, given too much power and unrestrained by free criticism, could become tyrannical. In a note to another correspondent, Colonel Edward Carrington, he expressed the hope that the people would always pay close attention to public affairs.

"If once they become inattentive to the public affairs, you and I, and Congress and assemblies, judges and governors, shall all become wolves," Jefferson warned.

In the decades after Jefferson had departed from this life, the Supreme Court gradually modified the meaning of the First Amendment. The Court said the Amendment did not cover "fighting words" or insulting accusations, which were not essential to the advocacy of ideas but were simply designed to be verbal blows.

Leo Pfeffer, in his book entitled *The Liberties of An American*, declared: "The exclusion of fighting words, obscenities, commercial frauds, and libels, individual or group, from the mantle of constitutionally protected speech is based upon the judgment that these types of utterances constitute so minor a medium for the communication of ideas that their social value is practically negligible, and the government therefore has almost unrestrained discretion to prohibit or restrict them."

Pfeffer and other authoritative commentators of civil liberties have acknowledged that the Jeffersonians would not go along with their notions. To the Jeffersonians, the government could rightfully concern itself only with deeds, not with words.

Jefferson wrote: "We have nothing to fear from the demoralizing reasonings of some, if others are left free to demonstrate their errors and especially when the law stands ready to punish the first criminal act produced by the false reasonings; these are safer corrections than the conscience of the judge."

But the judges disagreed with Jefferson. Over the years, their views have prevailed. In 1919, Justice Oliver Wendell Holmes delivered an opinion with the unanimous support of the Supreme Court that the federal government could put a man in jail for circulating dangerous ideas during a period when the United States was engaged in a war.

The Founding Fathers had given no indication that the First Amendment was not to be considered applicable during a war. But the Supreme Court upheld the conviction of a man named Schenck, who had attempted to persuade young men to refuse conscription in World War I.

Justice Holmes ruled: "When a nation is at war many things that might be said in time of peace are such a hindrance to its effort that their utterance will not be endured so long as men fight and that no Court could regard them as protected by any constitutional right. . . . The character of every act depends upon the circumstances in which it is done. . . ."

Later, the Court went farther—asserting that the First Amendment did not exempt from punishment the utterance of words having an evil tendency, uttered with an evil motive. Under the English common law, as Blackstone interpreted it, evil speech with an evil purpose could not be protected. Alexander Hamilton and his followers contended that the First Amendment was based upon English common law, and the Supreme Court acted on the Hamiltonian assumption in cases arising during World War I.

As a result of American participation in the war in 1917 and 1918, nearly 2,000 persons were given federal prison sentences for "impeding" or "attempting to impede" the war effort. In one case, five young men and a young woman were indicted for publishing abusive language about the government and urging reductions in the production of arms. The Supreme Court affirmed their conviction, saying that they had evidently acted with evil intentions.

In this case, Justice Holmes dissented. Speaking for Justice Louis Brandeis and himself, Holmes said: "It is manifest that there was no present danger of an attempt to overthrow the government by force. . . ." He felt that the defendants had a right to advocate their ideas vigorously, even in a period of warfare. His statements did not seem to be consistent with those he had offered in the Schenck case.

During World War II and in the Korean War (1950–

1953), the federal government and the courts showed much more respect for the Jeffersonian principles of free speech than in previous periods of international conflict. With the exception of the forcible evacuation of Japanese citizens from the West Coast in the early part of World War II, there were no mass roundups of people suspected of hostile attitudes toward American participation in these struggles. Freedom of speech and of the press, successfully maintained, did not hamper the American war effort.

In peacetime, the government has seldom attempted censorship or interference with newspapers or magazines, although government officials have often employed many devices to "manage the news" and keep the press from discovering what the government wanted to keep hidden. Whenever federal, state or local officials have attempted to curb the activities of the press, publishers have reacted strongly.

Publishers and editors are quick to cite the tradition of freedom established since the trial of John Peter Zenger, a New York printer who was accused of sedition in colonial times for publishing criticisms of the governor but was set free by an independent jury. The power of the press in politics since the United States became a free nation has kept it almost completely beyond the control of legislators and other officials.

From the beginning, there were differences in attitudes shown toward the press by the followers of Hamilton and by the followers of Jefferson. Hamilton said that liberty of political expression was "the right to publish with impunity, truth with good motives, for justifiable ends—though reflecting on government, magistracy, or individuals." Jefferson placed the highest values on "free argument and debate" and did not wish to burden people with the necessity of proving that they published their statements "with good motives, for justifiable ends."

"The good sense of the people will always be found to be the best army," Jefferson wrote in a famous letter to Colonel Carrington. "They may be led astray for a moment but will soon correct themselves. The people are the only censors of their governors; and even their errors will tend to keep these to the true principles of their institution.

"To punish these errors too severely would be to suppress the only safeguard of the public liberty. The way to prevent these irregular interpositions of the people is to give them full information of their affairs through the channel of the public papers, and to contrive that those papers should penetrate the whole mass of the people.

"The basis of our governments being the opinion of the people, the very first object should be to keep that right; and were it left to me to decide whether we should have a government without newspapers, or newspapers without a government, I should not hesitate a moment to prefer the latter. But I should mean that every man should receive those papers and be capable of reading them."

That last sentence of Jefferson's has often been overlooked or ignored by editors who point to his statement of preference for "newspapers without a government" rather than a "government without newspapers." Jefferson foresaw that a stable democratic society could not survive anywhere without well-educated people —people who had access to good newspapers, full of information and not merely designed to give entertainment or report sensational stories of crime and sex. He wanted every citizen to get substantial newspapers and to develop an understanding of the problems described in such papers.

In the twentieth century, with the expansion of technology and the growing complexity of problems, the question of whether ordinary citizens can get enough information and develop enough understanding to be effective decision makers has become one of the most difficult questions facing all those who believe in democratic institutions. Only a few publications seem to be equipped with enough staff members and enough resources to gather the essential information and to present it intelligibly to the public.

Americans struggling to understand and to support policies for coping with the challenges to democracy created by the revolutionary movements of this century have not been satisfactorily served by the press, radio or television. In many instances, the reporters and editors have not been able to get at the underlying causes of these revolutions. In other instances—such as the reporting of events in Cuba and Latin America generally—the press has not focused the attention of the public on the real dangers rapidly arising in vital areas.

Freedom of the press should not be regarded simply as a privilege conferred upon publishers, reporters, columnists, radio broadcasters and television station owners. It should be regarded as primarily a solemn responsibility—a liberty to be exercised for the sake of the people, to enable individual persons to be true citizens capable of making sensible decisions amid the confusions and conflicts of a new age of change.

Prior to the present period, the greatest threat to freedom of speech and freedom of the press arose in 1798 under the Alien and Sedition Laws. Under those laws, pushed through Congress by Federalists who were afraid of a conspiracy against the United States supposedly directed by French agents, many citizens were sent to jail for making critical remarks about President John Adams. Hundreds of Frenchmen, suspected of being plotters, were deported. Newspaper editors were thrown into prisons for writing "subversive" editorials.

Sanity was restored to the United States by Thomas

Jefferson and his associates. Campaigning against the restrictive laws that violated the Bill of Rights, Jefferson won the Presidency in 1800. When he took office, the Alien and Sedition Acts became dead letters. He set editors free, calmed the fears of the people, and restored the nation's devotion to the principles of free speech and freedom of the press.

Now the greatest threat to these freedoms seems to be the failure of many Americans to understand that such liberties are not to be treated as gifts, passively accepted. The rights of free access to knowledge must be demanded by newspaper readers, radio listeners and television viewers—or government will be completely in the hands of technical experts.

Some citizens who appear to be doubtful of the strength of American institutions are ready to limit freedom of the press whenever the phrase "for national security" is used by officials. Judging by the results of recent surveys, many young people are willing to acquiesce or to join in sanctioning such limitations on the free citizen's right to know what is happening and what governments are planning to do.

What does "national security" really mean? Does it consist of bombs and rockets, submarines and weapons of enormous power? Or does it depend upon respect for the constitutional rights and liberties of the people —and upon the spirit of the people themselves? These are questions all of us should consider if we want to be full-fledged citizens, now and in the years to come.

The line between anarchy and freedom is hard to draw. So is the line between the requirements of governmental secrecy and the requirements of a free press in a self-governing country. If we let the freedom of the press be limited too much, our basic rights will slip away from us.

Let us talk about these questions. Let us think about them. Let us examine them from every viewpoint—before it is too late.

V The First Amendment: The Right to Assemble, and the Right to Plead

IF YOU ARE invited to a political meeting in your town or city in the United States, you do not call your local police chief or a federal marshal or anyone else to ask whether you have a legal right to attend. If the meeting is sponsored by a group you regard as fairly engaged in a peaceful assembly, you know that you have a constitutional right to take part in it.

In a time when the United States is engaged in a struggle with Communism, you may check on the background of any group inviting you to a meeting. You may talk with a friend whose judgment you respect, or you may ask a newspaper editor or a neighbor about the proposed gathering, but you know that you are free to go—out of curiosity, out of a desire to see what may happen and what you may learn from the experience, or simply to assert your independence as a citizen.

The concluding clauses of the First Amendment— "Congress shall make no law . . . abridging . . . the right of the people peaceably to assemble, and to petition the government for a redress of grievances"— give broad protection to your right to join a gathering of people, to form a committee, to make a protest against a course of action to which you are opposed.

Every one of us has been urged at one time or another to speak up about something, to write to a Congressman or perhaps to send a letter to a newspaper praising or condemning somebody's speech or action as part of a group. The right to circulate petitions, to plead for a cause backed by many people or a handful of people, has become interwoven into the American way of doing things.

The fact that Communists, fascists, right-wingers or left-wingers have joined some committees or entered the activities of some organizations—such as some of the groups calling for the elimination of racial discrimination, for example—does not mean that Americans should be afraid to exercise their rights to assemble peaceably to discuss any subject. It does not mean that you or I should be unwilling to petition the government "for a redress of grievances."

If we have grievances, if we differ with Congress or the President or the Supreme Court about any question that seems important to us, we should consider it an obligation to voice those grievances. It is good for the government as well as good for the people to have criticisms and disagreements openly expressed. The sound of varying voices is one of the sounds always heard in a free and healthy society.

One of the errors made by the British cabinet and the English king in the eighteenth century was the rejection of petitions submitted by the American colonists. That was one of the contributing causes of the American Revolution. It was specifically mentioned in the Declaration of Independence.

Consequently, when the Bill of Rights was adopted, a section covering the right of assembly and the right to make petitions had a high priority in the eyes of Madison and Jefferson. Historically, the two rights were first treated as one—that is, the assumption was that the people ordinarily assembled in order to petition the government. In practice, the two sections have been treated separately.

The right of assembly may be used simply to give

vent to ideas without leading to petitions. The right of petition may be exercised independently of the right to participate in an assembly.

The word "peaceably" in the First Amendment has been interpreted to mean that legally constituted authorities may place some rules around these rights. Liberty does not mean lawlessness or anarchy. Your freedom to assemble a group does not mean that you may use that group to destroy the lives, liberties, or property of your neighbors.

A crowd assembling to lynch a prisoner held in a jail, or an assembly being harangued by a speaker obviously trying to start a riot is not considered to have the protection of the Bill of Rights. Courts have upheld the powers of governors, mayors, sheriffs, police chiefs and other officials to insist that the people assemble "peaceably."

The circulation of a petition seems to be, in its essence, a peaceful activity. Yet petitions have sometimes led to the adoption of restrictive or repressive legislation. Petitions have been used by minorities to get special benefits for themselves, and by majorities to establish excessive control over minorities.

During the stormy years when the question of slavery was shaking the foundations of the federal union, many petitions were sent to Congress, begging for an end to this shameful practice. The House of Representatives, perhaps hoping that the controversy over slavery would die away or disappear, adopted a standing rule (in force from 1840 to 1845) declaring that "no petition, memorial, resolution or other paper praying the abolition of slavery shall be received by this House, or entertained in any way whatever." The issue of slavery finally had to be settled in the blood and bitterness of the terrible war between the North and the South.

In World War I, persons circulating petitions against the recruiting of soldiers were fined or thrown into jails. In 1932, veterans who assembled in Washington to petition the government for payment of a bonus for wartime service were driven from their shacks and tents by troops and tanks of the U. S. Army. The veterans were regarded as a threat to the federal government, because some of their leaders seemed to be ready to lead an insurrection.

During the Cold War with Communism, which has been under way for many years, participation in certain assemblies and signing some petitions have been cited as evidences of disloyalty in charges brought against government employees and persons engaged in defense work. If an assembly seemed to be dominated by subversive groups, or a circulation seemed to be initiated by a Communist-front organization, anyone associated with such activities came under suspicion.

The principle of order and the principle of liberty have often come into conflict during this time of troubles. The government has the responsibility of maintaining order and upholding the form of political order established by the Constitution. Yet some citizens—sometimes only a few, sometimes many—invoke the protection of the Bill of Rights against the government in the name of liberty.

Having overthrown the rule of a royal tyrant, the founders of the American republic were deeply and constantly concerned about threats to the freedoms of assembly and petition. In a letter dated October 17, 1788, James Madison wrote to Thomas Jefferson: "Wherever the real power in a Government lies, there is the danger of oppression. In our Governments (federal and state) the real power lies in the majority of the community . . . the invasion of private rights is *chiefly* to be apprehended, not from acts of Government contrary to the sense of its constituents, but from acts in which the Government is the mere instrument of the major number of the constituents. . . ."

Madison was not at all sure that the Bill of Rights would be enough to save the individual liberties of people who ran counter to the will of determined majorities. In the letter to Jefferson, he said: "Experience proves the inefficacy of a Bill of Rights on those occasions when its control is most needed. Repeated violations of these parchment barriers have been committed by overbearing majorities in every State." He sponsored the federal Bill of Rights, however, because he thought it would be a factor in counteracting "the impulses of interest and passion."

Jefferson was far more optimistic about the long-range value of the charter of individual liberties than any of his associates. In an answer to Madison's letter, he pointed out that "though it is not always efficacious under all circumstances, it is of great potency always and rarely inefficacious. A brace the more will often keep up the building which would have fallen, with that brace the less."

The brace of the Bill of Rights has upheld the structure of American liberties, although the structure has often trembled and seemed about to fall in times of war or great agitation. Many of the struggles over the petition and assembly clauses of the First Amendment have been waged around legal definitions of "crimes of action" and "crimes of advocacy."

To sustain itself against traitors and rebels, the government has maintained laws severely punishing those who engage in actively aiding enemies of the United States. The Federal Bureau of Investigation and other agencies have been fairly effective in capturing saboteurs and spies, and in uncovering the work of traitors.

But the courts, Presidents, legislators and others have never fully decided (once and for all) on what should be done about people who simply get up in meetings and denounce the government, or people who carry petitions from house to house, demanding

71

new policies or condemning the official policies of the government. In the years of fear after World War I, when a great many Americans seemed to think that a Bolshevik revolution could be just around the corner, federal agents arrested hundreds of anarchists, syndicalists and other political radicals whose ideas supposedly had a "dangerous tendency." In many states, red flags were outlawed. Radicals were not allowed to hold meetings or spread their ideas without being subject to punishment. It did not matter whether their programs had any prospect of being put into action: they were regarded as guilty of "crimes of advocacy."

In the 1930's, the Supreme Court accorded much more liberty to radicals. The Court held that people could advocate almost anything if there did not seem to be any "clear and present danger" involved in such advocacy. A Communist who spoke to people on street corners, urging a revolution, could not be jailed unless it could be shown that his shouts would bring about a revolution in a fairly short time.

A decade later, when it became evident that Communist movements in a number of countries had been successful, the Court took a more severe attitude toward advocates of Communism and the supporters of other totalitarian doctrines. The Court finally established a new test for convicting defendants—the existence of a "clear and probable danger," which was somewhere between a "dangerous tendency" and a "clear and present danger." The Court said the government could restrain advocates of a dangerous doctrine when it seemed probable that some action would be taken to carry out the doctrine.

In wartime, as we have seen, the courts are generally willing to authorize the government to do whatever seems necessary to preserve the security of the nation. It is assumed that military victory for a country dedicated to the principles of liberty is essential for the future preservation of liberty. During the years of battle, the people have to submit to limitations of their rights.

Freedom of speech and freedom of the press were subjected to severe pressures when the United States entered World War I. There were millions of German-Americans in the country, and many of these people undoubtedly felt that the United States should have maintained its neutrality or should have aided Germany. The government under President Wilson decided that drastic measures were needed to prevent resistance to the military conscription program and to keep up the morale of the armed forces.

Under the Espionage Act of 1917—the first comprehensive sedition law enacted in the United States since the expiration of the Alien and Sedition Acts in 1800—heavy punishments were possible, as we noted in the preceding chapter. Prosecutions were pushed vigorously against hundreds of persons. Many publications were removed from the mails, on the ground that these publications contained dangerous ideas. Some German-Americans were suspected of engaging in secret movements, and their activities were closely watched by federal agents.

In World War II, freedoms of assembly and of petition were generally well protected, and relatively few prosecutions were brought under the Espionage Act. The country was much calmer, and the government was confident of the loyalty of nearly all of the people. Except for the removal of Japanese-Americans to detention camps, mentioned earlier, few signs of hysteria were shown.

During the Korean War, as we have noted, the right of assembly and the right of petition were maintained and respected. Of course, people who signed petitions opposing government policies or those who took part in Communist-front meetings were likely to encounter difficulties in getting jobs. The names of many groups were added to the U. S. Attorney General's list of "subversive" organizations—a list which was attacked as "unconstitutional" by some lawyers, but was used by federal agencies to check the backgrounds of prospective employees. In addition to Communist groups, the list contained the names of some of the extreme right-wing "fascist" organizations.

One form of assembly which aroused much controversy during the 1930's was the picket line. Workers protesting against low pay or employment conditions, or people who had joined labor unions and wanted the unions to be their representatives in bargaining over wages and other conditions stood in lines outside factories or stores. People who crossed these lines, including strikebreakers hired by companies, were subjected to boos, insults and sometimes physical violence.

The Supreme Court ruled in 1940 that picketing was a means by which organized labor expressed its views in a dispute. As a means of expression, the Court decided, picketing came under the protection of the First Amendment. It declared unconstitutional a law banning all picket lines.

However, the Court was naturally concerned about the rights of employers and the rights of persons who might want to cross the lines to get to work or for other purposes. So the Court held that all picketing could be prohibited in certain cases, when there were repeated outbursts of fighting, stone-throwing or other forms of violence. Peaceful picketing was protected, but not interference with the rights of others.

In other cases, the Court has declared that employers may not use coercive terms in speaking to their employees. An employer may exercise his right of free speech to make it clear that he is opposed to unions, but he may not threaten workers with the loss of their jobs or other penalties. The line between strong persuasion and a threat is sometimes hard to draw, but the Court has attempted to draw that line.

In all cases brought before it under the First Amendment, the Supreme Court has struggled to reconcile the principles of order and liberty—sometimes leaning toward the side of federal, state or local governments at the expense of individual freedoms, and sometimes favoring the maximum amount of liberty for the individual.

The right of association—a right not specifically stated in the Amendment—has been the subject of a number of legal disputes in recent years. The Supreme Court invalidated an Oklahoma loyalty oath which compelled all employees of that state to declare that they did not belong to any organization listed by the U. S. Attorney General as "communist" or "subversive." A person might have innocently joined such an organization without full knowledge of any "subversive" aspect of the group, the Court held.

The fact of membership in an organization by itself was not sufficient to taint a person with disloyalty or disqualify that person from employment, the Court ruled. The right of innocent association was held to be a fundamental liberty of Americans.

In the Dennis case, involving the conviction of eleven Communist leaders accused of conspiring to overthrow the government, the majority of the Court held that the Communists had done more than simply exercise their rights of free speech and assembly. The six members of the Supreme Court majority, led by Chief Justice Vinson, supported the ruling of a lower federal court that "the record in this case amply supports the necessary finding of the jury that the petitioners, the leaders of the Communist Party in this country, were unwilling to work within our framework of democracy, but intended to initiate a violent revolution whenever the propitious occasion appeared."

Justice Hugo Black, dissenting, declared: "The indictment is that they conspired to organize the Communist Party and to use speech or newspapers and other publications in the future to teach and advocate the forcible overthrow of the government. . . . I would hold . . . the Smith Act [under which the Communists were tried] authorizing this prior restraint unconstitutional on its face and as applied." Justice Black insisted that the defendants were actually found guilty of something they were supposed to be planning to write or publish, and he regarded a conviction on such a ground as "a virulent form of prior censorship of speech and press, which I believe the First Amendment forbids."

Justice William O. Douglas, also dissenting, recognized that the Court majority based its decision on the feeling that the Communist Party presented "a clear and present danger" to the United States. He said: "If we are to take judicial notice of the threat of Communists within the nation, it should not be difficult to conclude that *as a political party* they are of little consequence. Communists in this country have never made a respectable or serious showing in any election. . . . Communism has been so thoroughly exposed in this country that it has been crippled as a political force. Free speech has destroyed it as an effective political party.

"The First Amendment makes confidence in the common sense of our people and in their maturity of judgment the great postulate of our democracy," Justice Douglas asserted. "Its philosophy is that violence is rarely, if ever, stopped by denying civil liberties to those advocating resort to force. . . . The political censor has no place in our public debates. Unless and until extreme and necessitous circumstances are shown, our aim should be to keep speech unfettered and to allow the processes of law to be invoked only when the provocateurs among us move from speech to action.

"Vishinsky wrote in 1938 in *The Law of the Soviet State:* 'In our state, naturally, there is and can be no place for freedom of speech, press, and so on for the foes of socialism.'

"Our concern should be that we accept no such standard for the United States. Our faith should be that our people will never give support to these advocates of revolution, so long as we remain loyal to the purposes for which our Nation was founded."

In the 1960's, very few public officials seemed to share the confidence of Justice Douglas and Justice Black. Communists and other radicals were placed under strict limitations. In many places, they were not allowed to use public halls to voice their ideas. In many of the states, their leaders were prosecuted on charges of sedition.

Whether freedom of assembly and freedom of petition can be fully preserved in the coming decades will depend upon the judgments of juries and courts. If the juries and courts are dominated by men and women who feel certain that radicals cannot overthrow the government of the United States, it is likely that these freedoms will be preserved.

If the danger from Communist groups or semisecret organizations such as the Birch Society seems to be very menacing, it is likely that the activities of these organizations will be sharply restricted by legal action.

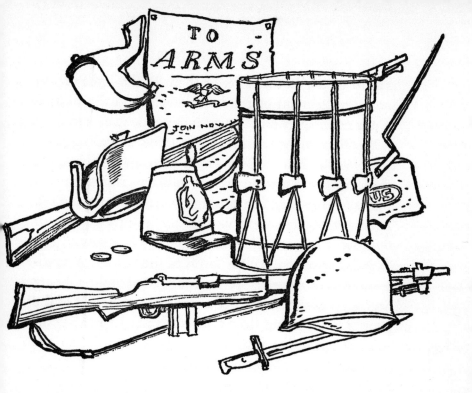

VI Second and Third Amendments: The Right to Bear Arms, and Civilian Rule Over the Military

Few Americans know the provisions of the Second and Third Amendments today, or the significance of their inclusion in the Bill of Rights. Yet these two Amendments contain important principles, important to us all. Let us look at them in the light of the long development of the human race and the history of our country as a nation of independent persons.

The Second Amendment was cited in 1962 by the organizers of Minute Men—men with some knowledge of firearms who formed private military groups to repel a possible invasion or uprising by armed Communists. The Minute Men were victims of the propaganda of right-wing leaders and were generally laughed at, but they did refer to the clear terms of the Second Amendment which asserts: "A well-regulated militia being necessary to the security of a free state, the right of the people to keep and bear arms shall not be infringed."

That is a rather revolutionary statement. In an age of jet planes, of rocket-propelled satellites, of hydrogen bombs and nuclear submarines and all the machinery of modern technology, the citizen's right to bear arms seems to have little relevance to most of us. But it is certainly possible that a nuclear war—if it did not devastate the earth beyond repair—might lead to a breakdown of modern military forces and a return to reliance upon a militia.

It is interesting to compare the clauses in Section 13 of the Virginia Declaration of Rights, approved by a convention in that state in May of 1776, with the provisions of the Second Amendment. The Virginia statement asserted: "That a well-regulated militia, composed of the body of the people, trained to arms, is the proper, natural, and safe defence of a free state; that standing armies, in time of peace, should be avoided, as dangerous to liberty; and that, in all cases, the military should be under strict subordination to, and governed by, the civil power."

That statement indicates that the body of the people, trained in arms, should defend and uphold the liberties of the people—against professional military officers as well as any other forces threatening their rights. Our ancestors had had enough experience with the standing armies of British rulers to know that professional military units would not hesitate to beat down the rights of citizens if given orders by recognized commanders. The leaders of Virginia, as well as the leaders in other states, did not intend to allow that to happen in the United States of America.

Fortunately for all Americans, General George Washington was imbued with that spirit. When he learned of plans to have the Army take over the federal government early in 1783—a movement encouraged by groups seeking a strong central power that could control the democratic tendencies already arising—General Washington spoke to his officers at Newburgh, denouncing the idea as "so shocking" that "humanity revolts." He urged his officers to remember that they had fought for the liberties of the people.

Washington urged his military veterans to prove to the nation their "utmost horror and detestation of the man who wishes, under any specious pretences, to overturn the liberties of our country, and who wickedly attempts to open the flood gates of civil discord, and deluge our rising Empire in blood." He went to the Continental Congress, put the plot bluntly before the members, and scotched it. The officers supported Washington, and the supremacy of civilian rule over the military was established as a fundamental necessity for the maintenance of the American form of government.

In our history, great generals as well as civilians have respected this principle. Because of this, we have never had a serious threat of military dictatorship in the United States. Generals and admirals have largely been content to serve the people, to accept honors and awards from Presidents and Congresses, and then to fade away quietly into retirement.

With the growth of a huge federal military establishment, staffed by men highly trained in many types of specialties, the army, navy and air force of the United States have grown more and more remote from direct connections with the people. The selective service system has been continued by Congress on a temporary basis, with almost automatic renewals whenever it comes up for consideration, but the number of young men taken by the draft is relatively small. Most of the men and women who enter the services now are volunteers, interested in the nuclear navy, space exploration, the air force or some other pursuit offering a professional career.

The principle of the militia exists, to some extent, in the National Guard units controlled by the states. Governors and state legislatures have held on to their Guard divisions, and have zealously defended them from proposals to merge them into one vast military organization. The Guard units are still supposed to represent "the body of the people," prepared to save "the security of a free state."

When officers in the Pentagon pointed to the inefficiencies in the National Guard system in 1957, state governors replied to the criticisms with hot words. One of the most articulate governors, James Folsom of Alabama, declared: "Only the foresight of our fathers in placing in the elected officials of the people the authority of administering the National Guard has, in my opinion, prevented a military dictatorship in this country."

Support for the Guard, Folsom said, "will be a strong blow for the perpetuation of democracy in our land and against that federal clique of brass and bureaucrats seeking complete control of all military forces of our country. . . ." Folsom's feelings were shared by other Southern governors, particularly after the racial conflicts in Little Rock led President Eisenhower to send federal troops into that Arkansas city. The President was convinced that the National Guard units there were not effective in maintaining law and order against mobs.

As the demand for equal rights has steadily increased among Southern Negroes, the Guard units in the Southern states have found themselves caught in the center of bitter controversies. Members of the Guard units have been uneasy about being used in the conflicts over the desegregation of schools and the other problems which have disturbed the South in the 1960's.

Southern Negroes, taking their place on an equal level with white men and women, have insisted that the Guard units must recognize that Negroes are entitled to the protection of a "well-regulated militia." The Guard commanders, often Southerners of the old tradition, have been forced to face the fact that the militia cannot escape from being involved in the civil rights struggle.

In the present age, when the United States has abandoned its tradition against a large standing army and when the militiamen are drawn into the turmoil over the rights of colored people, the provisions of the Second and Third Amendments are facing new tests. We do not know whether we can maintain these provisions —or our form of government—under the impact of the revolutionary changes occurring at an increasingly rapid rate.

General Dwight D. Eisenhower, in his farewell address as President, emphasized the dangers developing from the giant military-industrial complex which has attained such power in the United States. Since he left office, the power of the Pentagon has continued to expand. Under President Kennedy, more than 50 billion dollars a year were appropriated for military purposes—more than half of the total federal budget.

Eisenhower urged the people to be vigilant, to protect their liberties in the face of the expansion of the military-industrial establishment. Members of Congress and many newspaper editors took note of his warning. No one came forward with a plan for dealing with the problem. Perhaps it is a problem that cannot be solved under modern conditions.

What is the meaning of the Third Amendment at the present time? It says: "No soldier shall, in time of peace, be quartered in any house without the consent of the owner, nor in time of war but in a manner to be prescribed by law." The time in which we live is not a time of peace nor a time of war. It is a time in which changes happen so swiftly that the law seems inadequate to prescribe the manner in which new circumstances may be met.

Today our soldiers, airmen and sailors, our astronauts and nuclear submarine crews have ample quarters of their own. People are not asked to take them into their houses. But military jets fall from the sky upon the homes of civilians; sonic booms break windows and walls; radioactive fallout enters houses without the consent of the owners; and the lives of all of us are deeply affected by the giant military machines we have built in the hope of containing the forces of Communism.

In one way, we may have already abrogated the Third Amendment. In this time of tensions, we have taken the soldier into the house of the nation. We have depended more and more for our sense of security upon our military forces. We have poured billions upon billions of tax dollars into the building of bombers and rockets capable of wiping out whole nations overnight.

Our country has reached such heights of material prosperity that we have felt that we have much to defend. We have given much away to our friends and neighbors—and much to our former enemies and our possible enemies. And still the numbers of cars and refrigerators and television sets and storage bins packed with surplus foods have grown and grown and grown. We have felt that we must have immense military strength to protect all this for ourselves and our children.

To be safe, to be secure, we have made more weapons than we could ever use—more than we could ever intend to use. We have not desired to attack anybody. We have shuddered away from the brink of war. We keep building more and more monstrous weapons, hoping that every weapon will push war just a little farther away. We do not know what else to do.

Long ago, Alexander Hamilton foresaw what might come over us. In No. VIII of *The Federalist,* Hamilton put it in blunt sentences: "Safety from external danger is the most powerful director of national conduct. Even the ardent love of liberty will, after a time, give way to its dictates. The violent destruction of life and property incident to war, the continual effort and alarm attendant on a state of continual danger, will compel nations the most attached to liberty to resort for repose and security to institutions which have a tendency to destroy their civil and political rights. To be more safe, they at length become willing to run the risk of being less free."

"To run the risk of being less free"—that is the risk we are running in the twentieth century, as General Eisenhower stated so eloquently in his final speech as President. As a true successor to General Washington, Eisenhower spoke to Americans of our time and Americans of future generations. A man who had spent most of his life in the military service, Eisenhower was as deeply aware of the limitations of the military mind as he was of the dedicated devotion brought by many military men to their vital duties.

In his book, *The Right of the People,* Justice William O. Douglas defined the differences between military administration and civil administration. He underlined

Eisenhower's warning of the perils inherent in placing too many responsibilities upon the shoulders of military leaders.

"The military mind specializes in military strategy, the training of members of the Armed Forces, their deployment in the field, and their maintenance and support," Justice Douglas said. "Those problems require a regime of centralized control and unswerving obedience.

"The problems of civil administration are different. They require leaders who know people, politics, and the art of persuasion, and who have the ability to organize a community on a voluntary, cooperative basis. The military operates in a chain of command. There is little individual initiative at the bottom. The civil administration is decentralized with units close to the grass roots of the nation.

"The military operates through orders that allow little or no deviation. The civil administration invites criticism; and through the functioning of a free press and free debate among subordinates, the civil administration is adaptable to easy change and modification. . . . The military regime has the appearance of efficiency. But actually it is in a strait jacket of orders that can only be obeyed, not debated. The civil administration is far more flexible.

"The civil administration is the product of political processes rooted in the traditions of civil liberties and the rights of man. The military regime has a different expertise—that of war and combat. The civil administration brings to its task all of the great traditions embodied in the Bill of Rights. The military knows only short-cuts and substitutes."

Actually, of course, the bureaucracy is alike in both the military and the civil administration. The top military leaders may often be more flexible and more willing to try experiments than some of the civil administrators. But in general, Justice Douglas has brilliantly outlined the questions we must face when we contemplate the huge military-industrial machine now looming upon the horizon.

Do we have any choice about what course we will take in the coming decades? Is it possible to restore to "the body of the people" the defense of "a free state"? Can the efforts of a Secretary of Defense, the President, and others in our government keep the military machine under civilian control?

We can have a choice if we are willing to educate ourselves in the meaning of democratic principles in an age of change. With the increasing leisure we will have with shorter workweeks as automation increases, we will have the time to assemble, to debate these questions, to get members of the military forces into deeper studies of the meaning of freedom.

With the development of new technologies, we may be able to protect our national security with a small number of men. Millions may be released from the armed services to take their places in civilian life.

The civilian life must be a good life. It must be a vigorous, exploring, argumentative life—with many viewpoints fully displayed and fully defended. It must be a healthy life, grounded in freedom, with rights to education and decent housing and social opportunities open to every citizen, regardless of race, creed or color.

The "right to bear arms" should be interpreted as a right that carries an obligation to defend every man's freedom. Civilian supremacy over the military should be a supremacy freely recognized and supported by the military—as it has been many times by leaders ranging from George Washington to Dwight D. Eisenhower.

In such an atmosphere, the principles of the Second and Third Amendments will continue to live.

VII Fourth Amendment: Protection Against Unreasonable Searches and Seizures

IF A POLICEMAN wants to enter your house or search your possessions, he has to get a warrant—a legal document issued by a magistrate, authorizing him to do so. The warrant must be supported by an oath or affirmation by the person seeking such authorization, "particularly describing the place to be searched, and the persons or things to be seized."

In a federal case, the policeman is required to do this under the Fourth Amendment to our Constitution. This part of the Bill of Rights guarantees "the right of the people to be secure in their persons, houses, papers, and effects, against unreasonable searches and seizures." The Amendment also provides: "No warrants shall issue but upon probable cause, supported by oath or affirmation."

You cannot get a warrant to search someone's house or seize his private papers just because you have a suspicion that he has done something wrong. You have to justify the warrant on the basis of reason. If you are a policeman, you have to show a "probable cause" for action before the warrant will ordinarily be issued.

These provisions can be traced back—like the other Amendments—to the injustices suffered by American colonists. In the eighteenth century, the British king had permitted his judges to issue "general writs of assistance." These writs allowed the king's agents to search any place during the day or night in efforts to uncover contraband goods.

In 1761, James Otis argued in court, eloquently although not successfully, that such writs violated the rights of free men. Otis insisted that "the freedom of one's house" was an essential element of liberty and asserted that a man in his home should be as secure "as a prince in his castle."

The Fourth Amendment embodies these principles. It is similar in many ways to the tenth section of the Virginia Declaration of Rights, which contained these stern statements: "General warrants, whereby any officer or messenger may be commanded to search suspected places without evidence of a fact committed, or to seize any person or persons not named, or whose offence is not particularly described and supported by evidence, are grievous and oppressive, and ought not to be granted." Other state conventions adopted resolutions along these lines.

The Supreme Court has ruled that the person and premises of a person "lawfully arrested" could be searched for incriminating evidence without the necessity of obtaining a separate search warrant. It has assumed that police agents cannot make "lawful arrests" without reasonable justification.

Many legal controversies have raged around the Fourth Amendment, and today there are many inconsistencies in the attitudes of courts and policemen on what is permitted and what is not permitted under the Amendment. Inconsistency in judicial rulings in wiretapping cases has now led to a situation in which evidence obtained by state policemen—illegal in federal courts, if gained by wiretaps—may be used to get convictions in state courts, even though the state officers commit a federal crime by divulging intercepted communications.

The Fourth Amendment, like all the other provisions of the Bill of Rights, was designed originally to apply to matters coming under the jurisdiction of the federal government. After the Civil War, the Fourteenth Amendment was adopted—and this Amendment has been interpreted by the courts in some cases to extend the protections of the federal charter of liberties to judicial proceedings in the states. It states: "No state shall make or enforce any law which shall abridge the privileges or immunities of citizens of the United States; nor shall any state deprive any person of life, liberty, or property without due process of law; nor deny to any person within its jurisdiction the equal protection of the law."

Some of the Congressional leaders who took part in shaping the Fourteenth Amendment made it plain that they believed it would make the first eight Amendments in the federal Bill of Rights applicable to the states. Supreme Court judges have disagreed about this, but a majority of the Court held in a famous case decided in 1949 that the right of protection against arbitrary intrusion by the police was fundamental for the existence of a free society. Whether it was guaranteed by the Fourth or the Fourteenth Amendment, it could not be denied.

Speaking for the majority in the 1949 ruling, Justice

Frankfurter illuminated the whole concept of "ordered liberty." He wrote: "The knock at the door, whether by day or by night, as a prelude to a search, without authority of law but solely on the authority of the police, did not need the commentary of recent history to be condemned as inconsistent with the conception of human rights enshrined in the history and the basic constitutional documents of English-speaking peoples." (By "recent history" he was obviously referring to the police practices in Nazi Germany, where millions of people were taken away by night and by day to concentration camps and gas chambers.)

Justice Frankfurter went on to say, however, that unconstitutionally seized evidence could be used against an accused person in a state criminal court. According to the majority opinion rendered by Frankfurter, the remedy against unfair actions by state policemen lay in reprimanding the police officers or in permitting suits for damages against such officers.

One of the three dissenting Justices—Frank Murphy —found Judge Frankfurter's logic hard to follow or sustain. "I agree with the Court that the Fourteenth Amendment prohibits activities which are prescribed by the search and seizure clause of the Fourth Amendment," Justice Murphy said. "The conclusion is inescapable that but one remedy exists to deter violations of the search and seizure clause. That is the rule which excludes illegally obtained evidence. Only by exclusion can we impress upon the zealous prosecutor that violation of the Constitution will do him no good."

Justice Wiley Rutledge, another dissenting member of the Court, put his views in vigorous language: "As Congress and this Court are, in my opinion, powerless to permit the admission in federal courts of evidence seized in defiance of the Fourth Amendment, so I think state legislators and judges—if subject to the Amendment, as I believe them to be—may not lend their offices to the admission in state courts of evidence thus seized. Compliance with the Bill of Rights betokens more than lip service."

Do judges and policemen, state and federal officials who sanction wiretapping violate the spirit of the Bill of Rights—and specifically violate the Fourth Amendment? This has been a question argued bitterly in this century, with the increasing use of electronic devices which give some men the power to eavesdrop on supposedly private conversations.

Under the constitution of Puerto Rico, wiretapping is prohibited in definite terms. The Puerto Rican legislators agreed with the late Justice Oliver Wendell Holmes, who called it a "dirty business." Other state and federal judges have agreed with Justice Holmes.

Yet wiretapping in the United States has become a thriving trade. City detectives do it. State policemen do it. Federal agents engage in it. The general excuse is that clever criminals or persons suspected of subver-

sive activities may not be trapped unless their telephone wires are tapped or their conversations are
overheard.

The Supreme Court has not managed to develop a
firm policy on whether wiretapping should be outlawed. In a crucial case some years ago, the Court held
that the Fourth Amendment simply protected people
against physical entry into their houses or seizure of
something tangible. In this decision, the Court majority said it was permissible for federal officials to tap
wires and to testify in court on what had been overheard.

In giving the majority opinion in this case, which
was decided in 1928, the Chief Justice of the Supreme
Court—at that time William Howard Taft, a former
President, held this position—declared that the Fourth
Amendment referred only to searches for material
things. Mr. Taft said: "The United States takes no such
care of telegraph or telephone messages as of mailed
sealed letters. The Amendment does not forbid what
was done here [wiretapping]. . . . The evidence was
secured by the use of the sense of hearing and that
only. There was no entry of the houses or offices of the
defendants."

Justice Brandeis dissented powerfully: "As a means
of espionage, writs of assistance and general warrants
[of the kind not permitted under the Fourth Amend-
ment] are but puny instruments of tyranny and oppres-

sion when compared with wiretapping." Even when the tapping devices were used for a good purpose—law enforcement—he felt that they were dangerous threats to liberty.

"Experience should teach us to be most on our guard to protect liberty when the government's purposes are beneficent," Brandeis said in a statement which has been quoted by speakers and lawyers on many occasions. "Men born to freedom are naturally alert to repel invasion of their liberty by evil-minded rulers. The greatest dangers to liberty lurk in insidious encroachment by men of zeal, well-meaning, but without understanding."

Justice Brandeis did not see how the government could sanction the use of unethically obtained evidence. In another memorable statement, he said: "Crime is contagious. If the government becomes a law-breaker, it breeds contempt for law; it invites every man to become a law unto himself; it invites anarchy."

In 1934, the Congress placed in the Federal Communications Act Section 605, these words: "No person not authorized by the sender shall intercept any communication and divulge or publish the existence, contents, substance, purport, effect or meaning of such intercepted communication to any person." Not long after that, the Supreme Court said that "no person . . . shall intercept any communication and

100

divulge or publish [the information]" was meant to include a federal agent. The Court ruled that Section 605 prohibited the use of information gained by wiretapping as evidence in a criminal trial.

"Congress may have thought it less important that some offenders should go unwhipped of justice than that officers should resort to methods deemed inconsistent with ethical standards and destructive of personal liberty," the Court declared.

However, other ways of eavesdropping have been allowed. In a five to three decision, the Court refused to prohibit the use of a device called a "detectaphone," which was placed by police on a partition wall and used to hear conversations going on beyond the wall. The Court has also permitted eavesdropping outside open windows, and the use of secret microphones concealed in the clothing of undercover agents.

Most of the states have enacted laws against wiretapping. Congress has generally frowned upon it. Supreme Court justices have repeatedly expressed their distaste for it. But the United States Department of Jusice taps telephone wires in hundreds of cases, and has refused to take any action against federal, state, local officials or others who use electronic gadgets for a wide variety of purposes. ·

In a report issued in 1951, the Special Senate Committee to Investigate Organized Crime declared: "Wiretapping is a powerful tool in the hands of law-enforcement officers. Federal agents are seriously handicapped in their regular enforcement work by the legal restrictions which presently surround this valuable instrument of investigation. If properly safeguarded by the same restrictions that are imposed by law upon searches and seizures, wiretapping does not infringe upon the right of privacy of the honest citizen. Several States, notably New York, have laws which permit the use of wiretapping pursuant to court order and subject to reasonable safeguards."

What are "reasonable safeguards"? How can the citizen be certain that the "safeguards" are maintained? These are questions which have disturbed the legal scholars and judges who are opposed to the legalization of wiretapping.

Professor Louis B. Schwartz, in an article in the *University of Pennsylvania Law Review* in 1954, pointed out: "The chief difference between wire tapping and other forms of surveillance is the extent of its intrusion into the privacy of people who are not even suspected of crime. . . . Sometimes it is said that innocent people have nothing to fear from their conversations being overheard. But this ignores the nature of conversation as well as the fact that most people have some aspects of their lives that they do not wish to expose."

Under the Fourth Amendment, a search warrant has to be specific and restricted. The warrant must be backed by an oath or an affirmation "particularly describing the place to be searched, and the persons or things to be seized." This is not true of a wiretap on a man's telephone.

"Wire tapping is unavoidably a hunt for evidence, pure and simple, i.e., for incriminating admissions," Professor Schwartz wrote. "And since no one can forecast when the incriminating admission will be made, the hunt may have to go on for months, as against the specific and limited temporal authority granted by the ordinary search warrant for tangible things."

In an authoritative study of laws and procedures in criminal cases—a book entitled *The Defendant's Rights* —Professor David Fellman of the University of Wisconsin came to these conclusions: "It may well be that indiscriminate wiretapping would help the police to catch criminals, but so would listening in on confessions to priests, rifling of the mails, unrestricted search of private homes, the third degree, and many other practices which are now illegal.

"Whatever case may be made for wiretapping in restricted areas by police officers, subject to the strict limitations of a carefully drawn statute, wiretapping by private individuals seems to be wholly inexcusable, and ought to be made illegal everywhere, and punished where indulged in."

Whether state or federal laws prohibit or do not prohibit wiretapping, there seems to be little doubt that the practice flourishes in the United States and is likely to continue to flourish. Detectives tap wires, hoping to catch thieves. Federal agents tap wires, hoping to catch spies or other criminals. Privately employed agents eavesdrop on husbands and wives who suspect one another of infidelity. Agents for competing companies spy on executives of other companies, using wiretapping and other devices.

Since we live in an age of anxiety, in which many people are afraid of other people, eavesdropping has a deep fascination for government officials, executives in competition with one another, and many others in our society. Jefferson and Madison did not foresee the development of listening devices—and yet these devices often make a mockery of the provisions of the Fourth Amendment.

Perhaps the Amendment should be brought up to date. Perhaps our Constitution should contain a definite prohibition against electronic eavesdropping, just as the Puerto Rican Constitution does.

If a movement should get under way to modernize the Fourth Amendment, a national debate would undoubtedly occur between the proponents of "law and order" and the proponents of "the maximum degree of individual liberty." The tensions between the demands of national security and the requirements of personal freedom would come into the open again.

It is possible that such a debate would be healthy

for our nation and for all citizens. In the process of arguing over such questions, we would discover how much our freedoms really mean to us in a rapidly changing world.

VIII The Fifth Amendment:
The "Due Process of Law" and
the Right to Be Silent

You are accused of a crime. Your case comes up in court. Certain facts cannot be made known unless you testify. You sit in silence. Centuries ago, you might have been stretched upon a rack and forced to speak.

Or you might have been placed under oath by a judge, and compelled by that judge to answer any questions that entered his mind.

Your right to be silent, your right to what is called the "due process of law," your right to be tried only once "in jeopardy of life or limb"—all of these things are specified for your protection in the Fifth Amendment. In case after case, the courts of the states and the Supreme Court of the United States have maintained that these rights cannot be taken away from you or any other person under our Constitution.

The Amendment reads: "No person shall be held to answer for a capital or other infamous crime unless on a presentment or indictment of a grand jury, except in cases arising in the land or naval forces, or in the militia, when in actual service, in time of war or public danger; nor shall any person be subject for the same offence to be twice put in jeopardy of life or limb; nor shall be compelled in any criminal case to be a witness against himself, nor be deprived of life, liberty, or property, without due process of law; nor shall private property be taken for public use without just compensation."

It is a long Amendment. It has been the cause of many controversies. It has frustrated prosecutors, infuriated Congressmen, cost many people their jobs, and remained as a many-sided bulwark of individual liberty. It has been excoriated, misrepresented, denounced and defended. Its protections have been invoked by Communists, gangsters, businessmen, labor leaders, and plain citizens caught in the coils of the law.

Although its principles have been recognized in Anglo-American law for a long time, it did not appear in the Magna Carta or the English Bill of Rights adopted in Parliament in 1689. But it was written into the constitutions of seven of the thirteen original American states.

The eighth article in the Virginia Declaration of Rights in 1776—which was closely followed by legislators in Pennsylvania, Vermont and North Carolina—contains these provisions: "In all capital or criminal prosecutions a man hath a right to demand the cause and nature of his accusation, to be confronted with the accusers and witnesses, to call for evidence in his favor, and to a speedy trial by an impartial jury of his vicinage, without whose unanimous consent he cannot be found guilty, *nor can he be compelled to give evidence against himself;* that no man be deprived of his liberty except by the law of the land, or the judgment of his peers."

Virginians, Pennsylvanians, Vermonters and others who put together the Fifth Amendment to the federal Constitution were acting in the spirit of "Freeborn John" Lilburne, who had defied a Royal Star Chamber in England when he was tried in 1637 on a charge of printing and publishing seditious books. Lilburne said: "I am not willing to answer you to any more of these questions, because I see you go about this Examination to ensnare me. . . ." The Americans of the eighteenth century were determined to protect individual citizens from snares set by prosecutors.

Nearly all of the states in our federal union now have statutes guaranteeing a defendant or a witness in a criminal case the privilege of refusing to give testimony which may be self-incriminating. In New Jersey and Iowa—the two states without specific constitutional provisions on this point—courts have upheld the right, simply stating that it is a part of the existing law.

Dean Erwin N. Griswold of the Harvard Law School has described the Fifth Amendment in the federal Bill of Rights as "one of the great landmarks in man's struggle to make himself civilized." Supreme Court Justice Douglas has written: "It is our way of escape from the use of torture. . . . It is part of our respect for the dignity of man."

In cases decided in the nineteenth century, the Supreme Court declared that the privilege could be claimed by a witness as well as any accused person. Court rulings have stated that the privilege extends to all kinds of proceedings in which testimony is taken—including grand jury investigations, hearings by Senate and House committees, civil as well as criminal actions, and inquiries by administrative agencies.

It is a purely personal right, however. It cannot be used—under the interpretations of the courts—to protect an organization, such as a trade union or a corporation. It cannot be invoked to protect someone else; it can only be used as a personal privilege applying to matters of "self-incrimination." It covers anything that may *tend* to incriminate, as well as anything actually incriminating. "Incriminating" testimony has been held to be anything that may be damaging to a witness or might be held to be damaging.

Any person can voluntarily relinquish his right to invoke the Fifth Amendment. If he does not wish to take the stand, however, his failure to testify cannot be held against him in federal courts and in most of the state courts. It is true, of course, that members of juries are often prejudiced against defendants or witnesses who avail themselves of the right to keep silent.

The right of silence, however, does not cover everything; it covers only matters that might lead a witness or defendant to incur criminal prosecution. State, federal and local governments have obtained testimony by promising witnesses immunity—that is, freedom from prosecution for any self-damaging statements they might make in the course of giving evidence.

If a person refuses to testify after a grant of immunity, he may be prosecuted for contempt of the legal authorities granting the immunity. Legislators and other officials have been slow to extend immunity

111

privileges in many cases, however, because it has become evident that some guilty persons have bargained with prosecutors—giving evidence against others and escaping any punishment themselves.

In 1954, aroused by the fact that 317 witnesses had invoked the Fifth Amendment during 1953 before investigating committees, the Congress adopted an immunity statute with a broad scope. The Act gave immunity to witnesses called by either branch of Congress, or any joint committee composed of Representatives and Senators, in any investigation "relating to any interference with or endangering of, or any plans or attempts to interfere with or endanger the national security or defense of the United States by treason, sabotage, espionage, sedition, seditious conspiracy or the overthrow of its Government by force or violence."

The House Judiciary Committee recognized the difficulties involved in this type of legislation, in a report which stated: "The power to grant immunity is one of tremendous responsibility, the exercise of which must be guarded by discretion and wisdom. . . . It must at all times be the perfect medium whereby a true balance [is achieved] between the need and the right of the Government to obtain the necessary information to carry out its constitutional functions, and the constitutional right of an individual not to incriminate himself." In the eyes of some lawyers, the Act of 1954 did not achieve this balance.

Two years after it was passed, the Immunity Act was ruled constitutional by seven of the nine judges on the Supreme Court. Two of them, Justices Douglas and Black, felt that "the right of silence created by the Fifth Amendment is beyond the reach of Congress." The immunity granted to witnesses under the Act did not protect them from some repercussions of their testimony—the loss of their jobs, withdrawal of their passports, and other penalties. Such penalties, Douglas and Black insisted, were violations of the human dignity which was supposed to be protected by the Fifth Amendment.

Other major provisions of the Fifth Amendment are those stating that no man shall "be deprived of life, liberty, or property, without due process of law" and that no person shall "be subject for the same offence to be twice put in jeojardy of life or limb." Many volumes have been published on each of these principles, and hundreds of articles have been printed in legal journals, discussing the meanings of these magnificent statements.

What is "due process of law"? This question goes right to the basic nature of a civilized society. What does society owe to its members? What is "due" to each citizen in a free country with a tradition of respect for the individual person?

The ancient philosophers said that every man seeks justice. The object of law is to establish rules that treat every man fairly. The "process of law" is a cumbersome thing—a clanking machine, grinding ponderously, often immensely complicated. A natural yearning exists in man for swift and simple solutions to problems—to separate the innocent from the guilty, to make decisions with a minimum of confusion, to eliminate cloudiness and complexity.

Yet life is often cloudy and complex. Men cannot agree on exactly what happened on many occasions—who did what, who was responsible and who was not responsible. Men search for the truth, but each man has his own vision of the truth and his own way of stating what appears to be true.

The rules of a courtroom may seem complicated to the point of absurdity. But the rules are designed for a purpose: enabling the truth to emerge if the truth can be found, making it possible for men to be as just as they can be within their varying limitations.

Judge Curtis Bok of the Philadelphia Court of Common Pleas once wrote: "In the whole history of law and order the longest step forward was taken by primitive man when, as if by common consent, the tribe sat down in a circle and allowed only one man to speak at a time. An accused who is shouted down has no rights whatever. Unless people have an instinct for procedure their conception of basic human rights is a waste of effort, and wherever we see a negation of those rights it can be traced to a lack, an inadequacy, or a violation

114

of procedure." That is what the "due process of law" is all about.

The law is not designed to deal entirely with quiet, well-behaved people who invariably live up to their obligations, care for their neighbors, and understand what human dignity requires. The law must see to it that everybody—dope addicts, robbers, rapists, bomb throwers, all sorts and kinds of men and women—goes through the same process.

Some Americans seem to think that we must sacrifice some of our old liberties to preserve national security in a revolutionary age. Others seem to believe that individual citizens have rights and liberties—but no responsibilities. The "due process of law" provision in the Fifth Amendment is an effort to reconcile liberty and law, order and freedom.

Under this part of the Amendment, the government has to carry the burden of proving its case against a defendant beyond any reasonable doubt. The defendant does not have to prove his innocence. He is presumed to be innocent until he is proved to be guilty.

Under the "due process of law" provision of the Fifth and another provision in the Sixth Amendment (which we shall discuss in the next chapter), defendants can invoke the aid of the government to get witnesses to appear in their behalf. The government does not have to pay the expenses of getting such witnesses, unless it can be demonstrated that the defendant is without funds.

Forced confessions, obtained from defendants by police violence, are not acceptable as evidence. The "due process clause" of the Fifth Amendment has been held by the Supreme Court to bar any such police procedures.

The knowing use of perjured testimony by the prosecution was held by the Supreme Court in 1935 to be a violation of the "due process" clause. The Court said that defendants convicted by false testimony had been deprived of rudimentary justice.

In 1956 the Court ruled that a state had denied "due process" if it failed to provide a transcript of testimony, without cost, to a poverty-stricken defendant who contended that the transcript would show errors in his trial. Justice Black said: "There can be no equal justice where the kind of trial a man gets depends on the amount of money he has."

All of these rulings have apparently been intended to make sure that officials are scrupulously fair in dealing with persons who have been charged with serious crimes. The assumption underlying the Court's general attitude seems to be that an individual citizen needs the assurance of strict adherence to fair procedure when he faces the mighty power of a modern state or the tremendous power of the federal government.

The same principles apply in the "double jeopardy"

clause of the Fifth Amendment. The early leaders of this nation felt that no one should be faced by a series of prosecutions for a single act. The constitutions of 45 of the states have provisions banning "double jeopardy" similar to those in the Amendment, and in the other states the courts have declared that the common law protects a person from a series of prosecutions or multiple punishments for one crime.

If a defendant in a federal case is acquitted, the government has no right to appeal for another trial, according to rulings made by the Supreme Court. In a few states, however, the state may file an appeal if an "error of law" prejudicial to the prosecution was made. No state may attempt to set aside a finding of "not guilty" if it cannot prove that any major legal error was committed in the course of the trial.

Conservative as well as liberal judges on the Supreme Court have consistently asserted that the Fifth Amendment should be regarded as one of the indispensable elements in the maintenance of our liberties. Undoubtedly, some guilty persons have escaped punishments by hiding under the mantle of the constitutional privileges provided by the Amendment. But our legal system has been developed to preserve the dignity of every human being, even at the cost of letting some guilty persons escape from punishments due to them.

Justice Tom C. Clark, a conservative Texan serving

on the Supreme Court, said in 1952: "We must condemn the practice of imputing a sinister meaning to the exercise of a person's constitutional right under the Fifth Amendment. The right of an accused person to refuse to testify, which had been in England merely a rule of evidence, was so important to our forefathers that they raised it to the dignity of a constitutional enactment, and it has been recognized as one of the most valuable prerogatives of the citizen. . . . The privilege against self-incrimination would be reduced to a hollow mockery if its exercise could be taken as equivalent either to a confession of guilt or a conclusive presumption of perjury. . . . A witness may have a reasonable fear of prosecution and yet be innocent of any wrongdoing. The privilege serves to protect the innocent who otherwise might be ensnared by ambiguous circumstances."

Some circumstances might make a person appear to be guilty who was not actually guilty, and yet the person might not be able to give a full explanation of the circumstances. In that case, silence might be the best policy. This has been the view of many lawyers and judges.

In the twentieth century Justice Clark used the word "ensnared" in a way similar to the usage of the word "ensnare" by Freeborn John Lilburne in 1637. Both men took the view that a legal proceeding could not rightfully set snares or traps for persons participating in it. To be just, to be accepted by all men, a trial had to be fair.

Let us hope that the coming generations will have the devotion to justice which many generations in our country have shown. Let us hope that future Americans will recognize, as most Americans do now, that the members of a free nation are linked together in a community of persons. Each person, whether he is on the witness stand or in the jury box, whether he sits manacled to a guard or sits high on a judge's bench, has the right to raise a cry for justice—or by his very silence, to invoke a principle of justice.

Liberty and justice in a free society go together.

IX Sixth and Seventh Amendments: Fair Trials, and Trials by Juries

Guarantees of fair trials go back to the Mosaic code and Roman law. Under the rules laid down by Moses, two eyewitnesses had to agree on testimony concerning a crime before any accused person could be convicted of a major violation of a law. The Romans gave accused persons the right to confront their accusers "face to face."

The thirty-ninth article of the Great Charter of England—the Magna Carta—declared: "No freeman shall be taken, or imprisoned, outlawed or exiled, or in any way harmed . . . save by the lawful judgment of his peers or by the law of the land."

English judges and Parliaments went through a see-saw struggle for centuries over the question of whether the king was "under the law, not above the law." Chief Justice Edward Coke did not accept the right asserted by James I to transfer cases from the lawcourts and to act as judge whenever the king wanted to do so. When the king said that if the chief justice claimed that he was "under law" this was "treason," Justice Coke stoutly replied that the king "ought not be under men but under God and the law."

The principle was finally established that all men, whether they were princes or peasants, were under the law of the land. Jefferson, Madison and the other framers of the Bill of Rights contended that the Sixth and Seventh Amendments were vital to the preservation of this principle.

"In all criminal prosecutions, the accused shall enjoy the right to a speedy and public trial, by an impartial jury of the state and district wherein the crime shall have been committed," the Sixth Amendment begins. It also states that the accused person shall "be informed of the nature and cause of the accusation," shall have the right "to be confronted with the witnesses against him," shall "have compulsory process for obtaining witnesses in his favor," and shall "have the assistance of counsel for his defence."

The Seventh Amendment is much briefer. It deals with civil actions, and it says: "In suits at common law, where the value in controversy shall exceed twenty dollars, the right of trial by jury shall be preserved, and no fact tried by a jury shall be otherwise re-examined in any court of the United States than according to the rules of the common law."

Neither Amendment attempts to define what a jury is or how a jury trial should be conducted under the common law. In an opinion rendered in a case before the Supreme Court in 1930, Justice Sutherland wrote that a trial by jury "includes all the essential elements as they were recognized in this country and England when the Constitution was adopted."

Justice Sutherland said: "These elements were: (1) That the jury should consist of twelve men, neither more nor less; (2) that the trial should be in the presence and under the superintendence of a judge having power to instruct them as to the law and advise them in respect of the facts; and (3) that the verdict should be unanimous."

Although the Supreme Court has always held that these amendments assure an accused person in a federal court of a jury of twelve persons—the number required by the common law in the eighteenth century —the Court has also ruled that the states are free to vary the number. In 1900, the Court upheld a conviction made in a Utah court by a jury of eight members.

In many states, minor crimes and certain types of civil cases are handled by juries with fewer than twelve members. And the Court has ruled that states are not compelled to have jury trials at all in civil actions.

Under one provision of the Federal Rules of Criminal Procedure, approved by the Supreme Court, it is stated that "juries shall be of 12 members but any time before verdict the parties may stipulate in writing with the approval of the court that the jury shall consist of any number less than twelve." But such a stipulation is regarded by legal authorities as a waiver of jury trial, and this waiver can be made before or during the proceedings in court.

Unanimous verdicts are required in federal courts on all issues within the discretion of the jury. The rule of unanimity applies to civil as well as criminal cases. Lawyers and judges have occasionally expressed doubts about the wisdom of this rule, but it has been steadily upheld by the Supreme Court.

In Congress, in state legislatures, in committee meetings, in city councils, in courts (even in the Supreme Court itself), the verdict of a majority is regarded as binding. Why should juries in federal cases be required to come to unanimous agreement before their verdicts are accepted?

The insistence upon a 12–0 vote in the jury room is believed to be related to the necessity for establishing the guilt of a defendant beyond any "reasonable doubt." Since the jurors are selected with some care, it is assumed that all members of the jury are "reasonable" persons. If one of these persons has a doubt about the defendant's guilt that cannot be removed by the persuasive arguments of the other members, it is felt that a verdict should not be rendered.

Although there have been "hung juries" in a few notable instances, juries are nearly always able to arrive at unanimous decisions, although their deliberations may take many hours or a number of days. Consequently there is not an overwhelming demand for modification of the unanimity rule.

The states are not as scrupulous about requiring complete agreement by jury members. A jury in Montana may render a verdict by a two-thirds vote in civil actions and in all criminal cases except those involving very serious crimes. The New Mexico constitution authorizes the legislature to provide for verdicts by less than a unanimous vote in civil cases. Many other states have similar provisions.

The United States Supreme Court has not attempted to overrule any of these state constitutional provisions, holding that the Sixth and Seventh Amendment clauses concerning jury trials do not apply to the states. In fact, the Court has declared that the unanimous vote rule does not apply in state courts even when they are enforcing a federal statute.

The other major element in a jury trial is the presence of a judge, who explains the technical provisions of the law to the jury and may offer advice. A federal judge usually has much more control over a trial than a state or local judge.

Chief Justice Charles Evans Hughes once declared: "In a trial by jury in a federal court, the judge is not a mere moderator, but is the governor of the trial for the purposes of assuring its proper conduct and of determining questions of law. . . . In charging the jury, the trial judge is not limited to instructions of an abstract sort. It is within his province, whenever he thinks it necessary, to assist the jury in arriving at a just conclusion by explaining and commenting upon the evidence, by drawing their attention to the parts of it which he thinks important; and he may express his opinion upon the facts, provided he makes it clear to the jury that all matters of fact are submitted to their determination."

With all his prestige and power, however, the federal judge must always be conscious of the restraints upon him. He cannot go too far in his comments. He can indicate what he considers important in the evidence, but he cannot say that it points to a single conclusion; he cannot direct the jury to render a type of verdict that he may want.

Since the judge has a high degree of responsibility for seeing to it that the defendant gets a fair trial, he has to hold the prosecutor and the defense attorney closely to the rules of good procedure. When rhetorical, emotional statements are made by the prosecutor or any other lawyer in the court, he has to remind the jury that their verdict must be based on cool and calm reasoning related to the facts presented to them.

If a person does not want to have a jury trial, he can waive his right by stating in writing to the court that he does not wish to have one. The judge and the prosecutor must agree to conduct the trial without a jury before the waiver becomes valid.

Most of the criminal cases in state courts are tried before a judge. Many lawyers believe that their clients can get a fairer trial from an expert judge than from a group of inexperienced persons who may compose a jury. Many defendants are quite willing to dispense with the jury.

The problem of obtaining an "impartial jury"—required by the Sixth Amendment in cases where juries are used—occupies much of the time of judges, lawyers for defendants, and prosecutors. Prospective jurors are often questioned at length about their ideas and attitudes. Any number of jurors may be eliminated for "cause" by a judge or the lawyers for either side with the approval of the judge.

A certain number of "peremptory challenges" also may be used. The number is limited, and regulated by law. An attorney who uses a peremptory challenge to remove a prospective juror does not have to give any reason for doing so. He may simply act on "a hunch" or a feeling that the proposed juror will be prejudiced against his client. Prosecutors may also employ these arbitrary challenges without giving reasons.

An "impartial jury," the Supreme Court has said, is a jury "drawn from a cross-section of the community. . . . This does not mean, of course, that every jury must contain representatives of all the economic, social, religious, racial, political, and geographical groups of the community; frequently such complete representation would be impossible. But it does mean that prospective jurors shall be selected by court officials without systematic and intentional exclusion of any of these groups. Recognition must be given to the fact that those eligible for jury service are to be found in every stratum of society. Jury competence is an individual rather than a group or class matter. That fact lies at the very heart of the jury system."

There it is again—the emphasis on the individual. In every one of the Amendments known as the Bill of Rights, the spirit of respect for the freedom of the people is present—and the people are regarded as a collection of individuals. No person can be labeled, under our laws, as Rich Man, Poor Man, Catholic, Protestant, Jew, Atheist—or in any other way.

The jury system does not work perfectly, but no other system gives the ordinary citizen so much of an opportunity to participate in the search for justice. It is one of the democratic institutions which have proved to be useful through the recent centuries of man's development.

Millions of Americans who have served in the armed forces—which have their own courts, authorized under the Fifth Amendment—have realized the tremendous differences between military and civilian concepts of the administration of justice. This difference was clearly described by the late General Sherman, one of the Northern commanders who served with ruthless efficiency in the struggle between the North and the South.

General Sherman said: "The object of the civil law is to secure to every human being in a community all the liberty, security and happiness possible, consistent with the safety of all. The object of military law is to govern armies composed of strong men, so as to be capable of exercising the largest measure of force at the will of the nation. These objects are as wide apart as the poles, and each requires its own separate system of laws—statute and common."

Do the procedural safeguards of the Bill of Rights— the right to a speedy trial, protection against "double jeopardy," self-incrimination, coerced confessions, the right to confront witnesses "face to face"—apply to the members of our armed forces? It has not been finally determined whether these provisions are constitutionally required in military trials, although the military

code of justice does call for fair treatment of all accused persons.

"Military trials are trials where swift and severe action is often necessary for discipline," Justice Douglas
has pointed out in his book, *The Right of the People*.
"The military trial lacks the safeguard of the jury trial.
. . . Juries have sometimes inflicted injustices. But in
our long history they have usually brought to judgment
the quality of mercy that courts-martial do not often
show."

Justice Douglas has declared that scrupulous care
should be taken to restrict and confine "cases arising in
the land, [air], or naval forces" to "the narrowest limits
consistent with the constitutional purpose of giving the
Armed Forces disciplinary power over the troops."

"The contrary course would lead to a widening of
the jurisdiction of the military with a consequent loss
of liberty of the people," Douglas has asserted. "The
injury would not be the loss of jury trial alone. It might
be the loss of other constitutional safeguards. . . . In
World War I an attempt was made to enact a law
which would have punished spies by military trials,
the theory being that the entire United States was in
the war zone and that the establishment of martial law
was necessary for winning the war. The bill died in
committee after President Wilson announced against
it. He said: 'I think that it is not only unconstitutional
but that in character it would put us upon the level of

the very people we are fighting and affecting to despise.'

"A citizen who joins the enemy forces and invades the country to operate as a saboteur commits more than an act of treason; he violates a recognized 'law of war.' ... But for acts which add up to no more than treason, he should be tried not by the military, but by the civil courts, where he will receive the benefit of a jury trial and the special procedural safeguards erected around all trials for treason."

Section 3 of Article 3 of our Constitution defines treason in these terms: "Treason against the United States shall consist only in levying war against them, or in adhering to their enemies, giving them aid and comfort. No person shall be convicted of treason unless on the testimony of two witnesses to the same overt act, or on confession in open court." The courts have encountered difficulties in interpreting the words "adhering to their enemies" and "giving them aid and comfort." Consequently Justice Douglas and other jurists have felt that trials in civil courts, with a full and careful examination of each case, should be required.

The Army of the United States maintained for many years that it could subject to courts-martial former officers and soldiers who had been discharged and so were civilians, for offenses allegedly committed by them while they were in the military service. The Supreme Court in 1955 ruled that this provision in the Code of Military Justice was unconstitutional.

In case after case, the courts have resisted efforts by the military authorities to extend the scope of military jurisdiction. The courts have repeatedly shown their respect for jury trials as one of the signs of "the sovereignty of the people."

Alexis de Tocqueville, the great French writer whose study of the United States, *Democracy in America,* is as illuminating today as it was a century ago, spoke of the values of the jury system in these eloquent sentences:

"It teaches men to practice equity; every man learns to judge his neighbor as he would himself be judged. . . .

"The jury teaches every man not to recoil before the responsibility of his own actions, and impresses him with that manly confidence without which no political virtue can exist. . . .

"By obliging men to turn their attention to other affairs than their own, it rubs off that private selfishness which is the rust of society."

Any citizen, after he reaches the age of responsibility, may be called for jury duty. If you receive such a call, do not look upon it as an irksome burden. Look upon it as an opportunity to take part in the fundamental life of a free society.

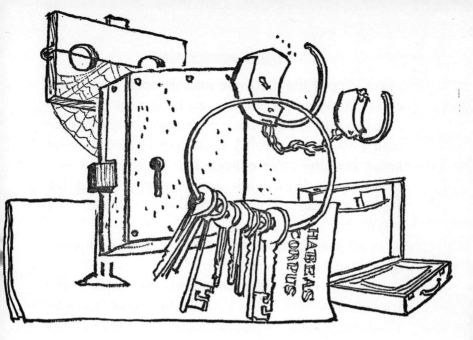

X The Eighth Amendment: Reasonable Bail Required — and No Cruel Punishments Allowed

W<small>HY SHOULD</small> accused persons have the right to obtain their freedom before a trial simply by posting a reasonable sum of money or property as bail? The authorities always take a risk when bail is granted. Sometimes spies and other persons have fled the country and forfeited the bail bonds posted by themselves or their friends.

Looking at the matter in another way, why should one man get out of jail because he can scrape up the required amount of money or property, while another man (perhaps innocent) must stay behind bars because he can't raise enough bail money? Can such provisions in the Eighth Amendment in the Bill of Rights be described as just to all persons seeking liberty?

These are questions with which lawyers and judges have long been concerned.

The idea of letting prisoners get out of jail before trial goes far back in the tradition of English-speaking peoples. The Bill of Rights requires our federal government to take the risk involved because the preparation of a defense against an indictment is obviously very difficult for a prisoner in confinement. With their determination to help the innocent and to advance the cause of justice, the leaders of our Revolution put the Amendment into the list of indispensable rights.

The Eighth Amendment states: "Excessive bail shall not be required, nor excessive fines imposed, nor cruel and unusual punishments inflicted." There are no definitions given of what "excessive" means or what "cruel and unusual punishments" are. These matters are left to the courts.

The authors of the Amendment were well aware of the fact that the English Parliament had denounced James II in 1689 for requiring "excessive bail . . . to

elude the benefit of the laws made for the liberty of
the subjects." The constitutions of all the states in the
American federal union (except one) now stipulate
that excessive bail is prohibited. The Eighth Amendment applies only to federal cases but the states have
followed the federal government in this instance as in
many others.

Granting liberty to a prisoner before trial not only
permits him to prepare his defense, it gives evidence
of the American belief that a person is presumed to be
innocent until found guilty. Society may try to make
sure that he will be on hand for his trial, but to hold a
presumably innocent person in jail pending a trial is
a form of punishment not to be inflicted lightly upon
an American.

In practice, the right to bail in federal cases is cov-
ered by Rule 46 of the Federal Rules of Criminal Procedure. Under this rule, a "person arrested for an
offense not punishable by death *shall* be admitted to
bail." An accused person arrested for an offense carrying the death penalty "may be admitted to bail by any
court or judge authorized by law to do so in the exercise of discretion, giving due weight to the evidence
and to the nature and circumstances of the offense."
After conviction, bail may still be permitted in certain
cases. The Supreme Court ruled in 1956 that bail "may
be allowed pending appeal or certiorari unless it ap-

pears that the appeal is frivolous or taken for delay." State courts have similar rules.

In many states, a prisoner who feels that he is being held under "excessive bail" may seek a "writ of habeas corpus"—freeing from bodily imprisonment anyone held without a just cause. Such a writ is an order signed by a judge or an authorized magistrate to set free quickly one who has been detained illegally. It requires that the body (corpus) of the person be brought before a judge for a hearing.

Although the right of obtaining a writ of habeas corpus is regarded as one of the greatest human rights by some noted lawyers and judges, it is not specifically mentioned in our Bill of Rights. The Constitution declares, however, that "the privilege of the writ of *habeas corpus* shall not be suspended, unless when in cases of rebellion or invasion the public safety may require it." In 1789, the first Judiciary Act gave authority to all federal courts "to grant writs of habeas corpus for the purpose of an inquiry into the cause of commitment."

Although all persons in the United States are legally entitled to "reasonable bail," poor people have a hard time in meeting the requirements of most courts. Successful gangsters who have amassed fortunes are able to post bonds of $10,000 to $25,000 in some cases, and so they are released on bail. At the same time, juvenile delinquents charged with minor offenses are kept in prisons for months before trial, simply because they can't raise the money to pay for their freedom.

In 1961, a *New York Times* reporter—Gertrude Samuels—discovered that there were 118,000 men and women in detention jails in New York, and most of them were there because they could not "make bail." Hundreds of these persons had been held for more than six months. In the Brooklyn House of Detention for Men—used as a jail for young men between the ages of sixteen and twenty-one—the average period of imprisonment without trial for each prisoner was 45 days. And these young men—like thousands of other prisoners—were packed into antiquated institutions designed to hold only two-thirds of their number. Conditions in the Greenwich Village prison for women were almost as bad, with some of the women "detained" for six months before their cases were heard.

Usually the prisoners who got released were those who could afford professional bondsmen—who supply "bail money" at a cost of 5 percent for the first $1,000; 4 percent on the second $1,000, and 3 percent for each $1,000 above that. These bondsmen often insisted on having collateral—savings bankbooks, stocks or other property—supplied by the defendants or their families. Most defendants apparently could not "make bail" if a judge required as much as $2,500; and 28 percent of defendants could not raise bail amounting to $500.

Disturbed by these conditions, Louis Schweitzer determined to do something about them. Schweitzer—a chemical engineer, who takes an active part in civic affairs—endowed a nonprofit research foundation to insure "equal justice under law" for the poor through study of criminal procedures, starting with bail-bond practices. He called it the Vera Foundation.

In October of 1961, the foundation launched the Manhattan Bail Project under the direction of Herbert Sturz. Students from the New York University School of Law, with supervision by Mr. Sturz, interviewed defendants brought into the Manhattan Criminal Court, and made recommendations to the judges on the possibility of granting paroles without bail to defendants whose records indicated that they were fairly responsible persons. In the first year and a half of this experiment, more than 400 defendants were released on their promises to return for their trials, and only 4 failed to keep their pledges. This was a better record of pledge keeping than the average record of persons who posted bail.

The District of Columbia and the municipal government of New York have announced plans to adopt policies based on the Vera Foundation's project. Attorney General Robert F. Kennedy, in a report on crime and poverty, adopted many of the recommendations made to him on the basis of the New York experiment. Mr. Kennedy has actively advocated federal programs to see to it that poor people get fairer treatment in the process of trials than they have received in the past.

In a summary of the results obtained by the Vera Foundation—prepared by Professor Charles E. Ares of the New York University law school, Ann Rankin, a sociologist, and Mr. Sturz—there are these hopeful statements: "The evidence gathered so far strongly indicates that parole can be utilized with safety in a substantial number of cases. With careful investigation and adequate notification and follow-up procedures, the overwhelming number of indigent defendants released on parole have returned. . . . Of course, the defendants recommended for parole have been carefully selected and poor risks have been avoided. But the requirements for parole have been gradually relaxed without adverse results. Over the next two years an attempt will be made to determine the maximum possible extension of parole. Available evidence at least suggests that the financial deterrent to flight has been overrated and that other factors—ties to the community—are really the effective deterrents. If this proves to be true, financial security should obviously play a secondary role as a guarantee of the defendant's return for trial." This summary was published in the *New York University Law Review* in January, 1963. Since its publication there have been indications that several major cities will try out a system of granting parole without bail to defendants whose poverty makes it impossible for them to post bonds.

Judges, lawyers and the public have long been fairly vigilant in opposing "cruel and unusual punishments" —prohibited by the Eighth Amendment. In the eighteenth century, Englishmen had turned strongly against such savage punishments as public whippings, disembowelings, beheading and quartering, burning alive, and other practices which had been authorized in earlier ages. The framers of the Bill of Rights sought to make sure that such practices could not be revived in America.

In the course of time, the ban on "cruel and unusual punishments" has been carefully examined and interpreted by the courts. The infliction of the death penalty for some crimes—regarded as cruel and barbarous by many people—has not been barred by the Eighth Amendment as the judges have interpreted it. A criminal sentenced to death may be hanged, shot, gassed or electrocuted. Prisoners may be kept in "death blocks" in prisons for months or years while their cases are being decided—and their prolonged suffering under the shadow of execution has not been regarded as a form of torture or "unnecessary cruelty."

After the invention of the electric chair, the question of whether death by electrocution was "a cruel and unusual punishment" came under consideration by the Supreme Court in 1890. Chief Justice Fuller handed down a decision finding it permissible. Judge Fuller said: "Punishments are cruel when they involve torture or a lingering death; but the punishment of death is not cruel, within the meaning of that word as used in the Constitution. It implies there something inhuman and barbarous, something more than the mere extinguishment of life."

The courts have gone into the subject of excessive sentences, and have decided in some cases that long sentences could be called "cruel and unusual." In Ohio, for example, a man was sentenced to ten years in prison for twice using a false name and address on a certificate of title to an automobile. The Ohio Supreme Court ruled that the sentence was excessive, and cut it in half.

Under the provisions of the Eighth Amendment prisoners have to be treated decently in jails, the courts have ruled. It is unconstitutional to subject them to physical violence or maltreat them as a matter of policy.

Since millions of persons in the United States have been accused of misdemeanors and crimes ranging from violations of auto traffic rules to major crimes such as assault and murder, the maintenance of the Eighth Amendment is highly important to a great many people. It is fundamentally significant for all of us, because it is one of the great pillars in our structure of justice under law.

Our concern about fair treatment for accused persons should not be based on sentimentality. It should be based on a realistic recognition of the fact that defendants—who are usually poor people and often are members of minority groups—do not have the large resources necessary to meet a government prosecutor in court on equal terms. Prosecutors are often obsessed with "winning cases" and often forget that a trial is not a game or a contest but a way of seeing to it that the guilty are punished and the innocent are set free.

Many poor persons who are brought into court plead guilty because they are confused or have no idea of how they may establish their innocence. The Eighth Amendment, interpreted to include the idea of parole without posted bonds for persons whose records indicate that they are trustworthy, gives many such persons a chance to prepare their defenses outside the oppressive shadows of prison walls.

XI Ninth and Tenth Amendments: Rights and Powers Retained by the People and the States

Governments get their just powers from the consent of the governed. If we, the people, do not give our consent to the actions of our governors, they must change their policies. The men who made our Constitution and the Bill of Rights hammered these points into the minds of their fellow Americans. These ideas must be understood and supported by each new generation.

In the eyes of Madison, Jefferson, Hamilton and other leaders of our Revolution, the great charters they wrote in their time simply indicated *some* of the rights and powers of the people and the states. They expected other generations to draw out the meanings of these reserved rights and potentialities when crises had to be faced.

The Ninth Amendment is short and straight: "The enumeration in the Constitution of certain rights shall not be construed to deny or disparage others retained by the people." The Tenth is equally direct: "The powers not delegated to the United States by the Constitution, nor prohibited by it to the states, are reserved to the states respectively, or to the people."

James Madison said: "If we advert to the nature of republican government, we shall find that the censorial power is in the people over the government, and not in the government over the people." The Ninth Amendment got into the Bill of Rights because Madison and his associates were devoted to that idea. The Tenth Amendment was designed to satisfy those who sought to protect the powers of the states.

The participants in the Constitutional Convention of 1787 regarded themselves as representatives of the people—and of the states composing the federal union. Although the Preamble to the Constitution referred only to "We, the people of the United States," the second section of Article I referred to "the several states" and the Constitution was regarded as an agreement among the states as well as a charter "ordained" by the people.

Justice William J. Brennan, Jr., of the Supreme Court has pointed out: "The constitutions of the original states anticipated the national Constitution in declaring the doctrine that there are human liberties which are inalienable. This doctrine has ever since been the center and core of the American idea of limited government. The government of each state was the creation of the people of the state; the source of power was the people of that state. The only end and aim of government was to secure the people in their natural and civil rights."

One of our first Presidents, John Quincy Adams, asserted that the division of powers between the federal authorities and the state authorities gave Americans "the most complicated government on the face of the globe." This complicated form of government suffered a bloody breakdown in 1861, when some states announced that they had the power to leave the federal union. These states seceded and formed the Confederacy; it took four years of battle for the forces led by President Lincoln to re-establish the principle of federal union.

Many of the leaders in the Southern states, although

they accepted the military defeat, did not believe that the federal government could supersede or override the states in many fields. The struggle over States' rights has continued into the twentieth century, and has led to clashes between federal and state authorities in a number of areas.

After the end of the 1861–1865 conflict, the Thirteenth Amendment was proposed and adopted to express the determination of the victors to wipe out slavery. The Amendment stated: "Neither slavery nor involuntary servitude, except as a punishment for crime whereof the party shall have been duly convicted, shall exist within the United States, or any place subject to their jurisdiction. Congress shall have power to enforce this article by appropriate legislation." That Amendment was approved by the state legislatures with very little opposition.

Congress passed legislation giving the freed Negroes all the legal protections accorded to white citizens. But doubts arose about some of these laws, and there was a strong demand for another constitutional amendment to clear away the legal issues. This Amendment —which became the Fourteenth added to the Constitution—will be discussed in detail in a later chapter. Let us note here that it stirred up a storm because it was considered a threat to "the reserved powers of the States."

When Congress debated the various proposals that

later were revised into the Fourteenth Amendment, the arguments were hot and heavy. Senator Browning of Illinois predicted dire developments: "If the proposed amendments of the Constitution be adopted, new and enormous power will be claimed and exercised by Congress, as warranted by such amendments, and the whole structure of our Government will perhaps gradually but yet surely be revolutionized. And so will the Judiciary. If the proposed amendments be adopted, they may and certainly will be used substantially to annihilate the State judiciaries. . . . Be assured, if this new provision be engrafted in the Constitution it will, in time, change the entire texture and structure of our Government, and sweep away all the guarantees of safety devised and provided by our patriotic sires of the revolution. . . ." Browning was not alone in expressing such fears.

The proposals he viewed with such alarm, however, were more drastic than those the Fourteenth Amendment contained in its final form. One proposal stated: "Congress shall have power to make all laws which shall be necessary and proper to secure to citizens of each State all privileges and immunities of citizens in the several States . . . and to all persons in the several States equal protection in the rights of life, liberty and property." The language was changed before the Amendment went to the states for approval.

As it was when adopted and as it stands today, the

first section of the Fourteenth Amendment reads: "No state shall make or enforce any law which shall abridge the privileges or immunities of citizens of the United States; nor shall any state deprive any person of life, liberty, or property without due process of law; nor deny to any person within its jurisdiction the equal protection of the law." Traditionally, the states had the powers to make laws affecting the lives, liberties and property of their citizens. The Amendment asserted that they could not use these powers to "abridge the privileges or immunities of citizens of the United States" nor refuse to grant anyone "equal protection of the law."

Even in its modified form, the Amendment was resisted as an assault upon the "sovereign powers" of the states. Its very existence was denounced as a betrayal of the principles of the Founding Fathers. But the resistance and the outcries died down when state authorities discovered that the Supreme Court was generally disposed to interpret the Amendment very cautiously.

Although the Civil War had been fought primarily over the question of whether the federal union had supreme power on fundamental issues over the states, the Court hesitated to act upon the implications of the Union victory. For nearly thirty years—from 1868 to 1897—the Court saw its role as that of a judicial "bal-

148

ancing body," restoring the legal equilibrium between the states and the national government.

The judges were extremely reluctant to declare acts of state legislatures unconstitutional and seldom did so in the years immediately following the Civil War.

But in the 1870's and 1880's the nation changed rapidly from the agrarian community on which Jefferson and Madison had based their hopes into the huge industrial country visualized by Alexander Hamilton. The change in the economic situation produced drastic changes in the lives of millions of Americans, who left the farms and became workers in the factories and mills. State legislatures came under increasing pressures to reglate the power of the new industrial organizations.

Lawyers for the railroads and other large corporations succeeded in getting the Supreme Court to strike down state regulations aimed at controlling them. Such state laws were branded as "socialistic measures." A corporation was defined legally as a "person," and then the first section of the Fourteenth Amendment was said to apply to such "persons." To repeat, that section read: "No state shall make or enforce any law which shall abridge the privileges or immunities of citizens of the United States; nor shall any state deprive any person of life, liberty, or property without due process of law; nor deny to any person within its jurisdiction the equal protection of the law."

149

No one quite knew what some of the phrases in this section meant, and judges and lawyers have worried over them for nearly a century with varying interpretations. The first great constitutional case carried to the Supreme Court on the basis of the Fourteenth Amendment was a suit brought by a group of New Orleans butchers against an act of a Louisiana legislature. The act had granted a monopoly in livestock slaughtering to one New Orleans corporation. The butchers contended that they had been deprived of some of the "privileges" and "immunities" guaranteed to them as United States citizens—specifically, the privileges of engaging in the slaughterhouse business in New Orleans with "immunities" against state prosecution.

The Honorable John A. Campbell, a former Supreme Court justice, was the lawyer for the butchers. He delivered a powerful statement to the Court, asserting that the Fourteenth Amendment had brought all the rights of man—including the right to engage in any lawful occupation—within the scope of federal law.

In a decision handed down in 1873, four of the nine judges shared Campbell's view that the Amendment called for a revolutionary alteration in the nation-state relationship with the Supreme Court as the final arbiter. Five judges, constituting a majority, said the state of Louisiana had a right to determine who might operate slaughterhouses in New Orleans. The "privileges" of United States citizenship did not give any butcher

150

a constitutional right to engage in the slaughterhouse trade, the majority stated.

The "privileges or immunities" clause was construed by the Court majority to cover only certain special rights, such as the right to travel freely through the country, the "right to use the navigable waters of the United States," and a few other simple rights of that nature. The majority said that, with a few exceptions, "the entire domain of the privileges and immunities of the citizens of the states . . . lay within the constitutional and legislative power of the states, and without that of the federal government." They did not think the Fourteenth Amendment was intended "to transfer the security and protection of all the civil rights . . . from the states to the federal government."

While the Ninth and Tenth Amendments were not specific in outlining what powers were reserved to the states and the people, the majority of Supreme Court judges in the latter half of the nineteenth century and in the first quarter of this century held fairly solidly to the idea that many areas of action were still within the jurisdictions of state governments. In the last thirty-six years the Court has moved rather rapidly in approving extensions of power for the national government and limiting the powers of state governments.

In many areas of personal activity, however, state laws still apply. When a child is born, the state or a local authority constituted by a state law registers the birth. When young people want to get married, they have to comply with the state regulations to obtain a license. In many trades, state licenses are required.

School boards operate under state laws. Divorce suits and ordinary criminal and civil cases are handled by state courts. States build highways, control water supplies, provide general relief for the poor, operate hospitals for paupers and insane persons, control the licensing of drivers and motorcars, manage colleges and universities, have military units and air patrols, and have police forces.

In taxation, state governments and the federal government sometimes overlap. All citizens who earn certain amounts of money are required to pay federal income taxes. Citizens in many states are also required to pay state income taxes on the same income. The tax systems are administered separately, and violations of state and federal laws are tried in separate courts—although in some cases the laws are virtually identical.

Article I, Section 8, of the Constitution of the United States describes the numerous powers granted to the federal Congress, and the states are not allowed to enter those areas. Congress has power to impose and collect federal taxes, to borrow money on the credit of the United States, to regulate commerce with foreign nations and among the several states, to coin money, to declare war, and to do many other things which the states are not empowered to do.

In the concluding paragraph of this section of the Constitution there is a statement which has been interpreted by the courts to give Congress enormous powers. This statement says that Congress shall have the right "to make all laws which shall be necessary and proper for carrying into execution" the powers specifically enumerated.

With the increased mobility of the American people —the average family moves every four years—and with the development of national networks of communication and transportation, state boundaries have less and less practical significance. Our country was originally established as a federal union of states, with functions divided between the central organs of government and the state organs. Now it is becoming a nation unified by the demands of its people for an affluent way of life under national laws and a national code of behavior.

Many of the powers once reserved to the states are being transferred to the federal government. Nothing in sight seems likely to reverse this process.

In the following pages, we shall examine some of the explosive elements in this revolutionary situation.

XII The Bill of Rights Applied
to the States

To support the right of a Negro student to enroll in the University of Mississippi, the President of the United States in 1962 mobilized thousands of soldiers—and the nation generally accepted his action. In 1963, additional thousands of troops stood ready to come to the aid of Negro citizens seeking to break down segregation patterns in the city of Birmingham. The President urged state and city authorities to meet the reasonable requests of the Negroes and to handle the situation without resort to military force. But again he indicated that he was ready to intervene with federal tanks, planes and men if that became necessary.

Negroes had hoped that the passage of the Thirteenth, Fourteenth and Fifteenth Amendments after the tragic Civil War would give them all the rights and privileges of other citizens. But the states of the South, seeing the demands of the Negroes as a threat to the separation of the white and colored races, used every power they could summon to keep the federal government from taking control of civil rights and civil liberties.

In 1875 the United States Congress passed a series of "civil rights acts" which were intended to give the Negroes full equality with other Americans. But the Supreme Court held that the "enforcement clause" of the Fourteenth Amendment did not authorize Congress to take action against transgressions by "private persons" on the rights of individuals, Negro or white. In an 1883 decision, the Court held that the protection of civil rights was vested in the states and not in the national government, and insisted that the Fourteenth Amendment had made no essential change in this field of legislation.

There seems little doubt that the framers of the Fourteenth Amendment felt that it would apply the provisions of the Bill of Rights to cases arising under state laws, but they did not make their feelings clear enough for the judges who were on the supreme bench during the latter years of the nineteenth century.

The Amendment said nothing about "separate but

equal" facilities being provided for members of the white and colored groups on railroad trains or in educational systems. Yet the Supreme Court ruled in 1896 that separating Negroes from whites in railroad coaches did not violate the Amendment's clause calling for "equal protection of the laws" for all citizens. So long as the accommodations were "substantially equal," the Court felt that fair treatment was being given.

The "separate but equal" doctrine was maintained for more than fifty years. In 1950, however, the Court began to swing toward a different position. It ordered a Negro admitted to the University of Texas Law School despite the fact that the state legislature had provided a separate law school for colored students. The Court said the separate law school was not on the same level with the law school available to white students; the school for Negroes did not have the same faculty, the same type of library, the same prestige or influence as the University of Texas Law School. In effect, the Court acknowledged that it was impossible for the state to produce a "separate but equal" law school for the Negroes.

Then came the unanimous Court decision of 1954, declaring that segregated schooling was "inherently unequal." The Court endorsed a finding by social psychologists and lower-court judges that legally sanctioned segregation in the public schools tended to hold back "the educational and mental development of

157

Negro children." That was the first in a series of decisions outlawing segregation in many areas of activity.

In the twentieth century, many of the essential elements of the federal Bill of Rights have been brought within the Fourteenth Amendment and made applicable to the states by a process described by Justice Benjamin Cardozo as a "process of absorption." Justice Cardozo said in an opinion rendered in 1937: "The process of absorption has had its source in the belief that neither liberty nor justice would exist if . . . [those guarantees] were sacrificed."

Justice William J. Brennan, Jr., in an address delivered in February, 1961, at the New York University School of Law, expressed his belief that all of the major provisions of the First Amendment had been extended to the states. He said: "As recently as 1922, the Court had held that the Fourteenth Amendment did not make the protections of the First Amendment binding on the States. Since 1925, however, decisions have extended against state power the amendment's protections for religion, speech, press, assembly, and petition. . . .

"Besides the First Amendment guarantees, only three specifics of the federal list, as such, have so far been held to be absorbed by the due process [of law] clause. Due process applies to the states the Fifth Amendment's requirement that 'just compensation' shall be paid for private property taken for public use. . . . Due process requires the states to appoint counsel for an accused charged with an offense punishable by death, in accordance with the Sixth Amendment's requirement that an accused shall have 'the assistance of counsel for his defense.' Finally, due process applies to the states the Fourth Amendment's guarantees against unreasonable searches and seizures. After holding in 1914 that the Fourth Amendment was not directed against state officials, the Court in 1949 held that 'the security of one's privacy against arbitrary intrusion by the police . . . is . . . implicit in the 'concept of ordered liberty' and as such enforceable against the States through the Due Process Clause.'

"But considerations of federalism have thus far overborne the arguments in favor of the extension, as such, of the rest of the list."

Justice Brennan went on to say: "It is reason for deep satisfaction that many of the states effectively enforce the counterparts in state constitutions of the specifics of the Bill of Rights. Indeed, some have been applied by states to an extent beyond that required of the national government by the corresponding federal guarantee. But too many state practices fall far short. Far too many cases come from the states to the Supreme Court presenting dismal pictures of official lawlessness, of illegal searches and seizures, illegal detentions attended by prolonged interrogation and coerced admissions of guilt, of the denial of counsel, and downright brutality. Judicial self-restraint which defers too much to the sovereign powers of the states and reserves judicial intervention for only the most revolting cases will not serve to enhance Madison's priceless gift of 'the great rights of mankind secured under this Constitution.' For these secure the only climate in which the law of freedom can exist."

The Supreme Court came very close to incorporating the entire Bill of Rights into an interpretation of the Fourteenth Amendment given by four of the nine judges in the Adamson v. California case in 1947. A man named Adamson, convicted of murder in a California court, appealed to the Supreme Court, claiming that he had not received a fair trial and invoking the "due process of law" clause of the Amendment. The majority of the Court said: "The due process clause of the Fourteenth Amendment, however, does not draw all the rights of the Federal Bill of Rights under its protection. . . ."

Justice Hugo Black, speaking for the minority of four judges, asserted that the Amendment had made all the provisions of the charter of liberties effective in state courts as well as federal ones. Black said that his study of the debate over the passage of the Amendment had convinced him that "one of the chief objects that the provisions of the Amendment's first section, separately, and as a whole, were intended to accomplish was to make the Bill of Rights applicable to the

160

states. . . . This historical purpose has never received full consideration or exposition in any opinion of this Court interpreting the Amendment. . . .

"I fear to see the consequences of the Court's practice of substituting its own concepts of decency and fundamental justice for the language of the Bill of Rights," Black said. "I would follow what I believe was the original purpose of the Fourteenth Amendment—to extend to all the people of the nation the complete protection of the Bill of Rights. To hold that this Court can determine what, if any, provisions of the Bill of Rights will be enforced, and if so to what degree, is to frustrate the great design of a written Constitution."

Justice Frank Murphy supported Black's position strongly, and carried the argument a step further: "I agree that the specific guarantees of the Bill of Rights should be carried over intact into the first section of the Fourteenth Amendment. But I am not prepared to say that the latter is entirely and necessarily limited by the Bill of Rights. Occasions may arise where a proceeding falls so far short of conforming to fundamental standards of procedure as to warrant constitutional condemnation in terms of a lack of due process, despite the absence of a specific provision in the Bill of Rights."

As we have noted, the Court in recent decades has disapproved a sizable number of state actions—knocking down the state laws forbidding peaceful picketing, laws requiring union organizers to register with state authorities, disapproving state court contempt proceedings against persons who were accused of using the press to influence judicial procedures, and wiping out state sedition laws by claiming that Congress had superseded such laws by national legislation.

The Court has also increased the number of ways in which the states are bound to follow federal standards in their general criminal procedures, as we indicated in an earlier chapter.

In affirming the constitutional protections afforded to Negroes in their struggle for equality, the Court has been zealous in recent years. It has struck down local laws aimed at preventing the assembly of Negroes who wished to hold "protest meetings" against discriminatory practices. It has invalidated various legislative measures used in the Southern states to keep Negroes from voting.

Although it has moved steadily in the direction of a federal responsibility for the maintenance and expansion of individual liberties, the Court has not moved fast enough to meet the urgent needs of modern society —in the opinion of one of its current members, Justice Douglas, and in the opinion of other critics. The upholders of traditional States' rights doctrines, on the other hand, have become so alarmed that they have launched a movement to get approval for a constitutional movement establishing a new court—a Court of the Union, composed of the chief justices of the fifty states, with sole power to rule on constitutional questions.

"The central problem of the age is the scientific revolution and all the wonders and the damage it brings," Justice Douglas said in a lecture in 1962. "The scientific revolution displaces men and substitutes the machine with the result that we have the promise of a permanent surplus of unemployed people.

"The liberal-conservative dichotomy of the 1930's is obsolete. What are the Rights of Men against the machine as it becomes increasingly important? What do we substitute for work—as a discipline, and as a means of distributing income? What Bill of Rights does man now need to keep a modicum of liberty? The forces allied against the individual have never been greater. The scientific revolution makes production and consumption the ends of society. Yet are they 'the pursuit of happiness'? The scientific revolution teaches conformity in a myriad of ways. The scientific revolution produces, indeed, a vast interdependency among people. Where in this tightly knit regime is man to find liberty?"

In this address, Justice Douglas said the need for procedural due process of law was greater today than in the eighteenth century when the Bill of Rights was adopted.

"If the Bill of Rights were being written today, it certainly would provide people with protection against poisoning by insecticides—one of America's acute problems, as Rachel Carson shows in her book, *Silent Spring*," Justice Douglas declared.

"If the Bill of Rights were being written today, it also would encompass some of the recurring evils arising out of the vast exercise of authority through the administrative agency. Thus in one State an administrative board of three may, on a majority vote, sterilize a person without notice, without an opportunity to be heard, without an application being made to any other tribunal or agency. One state provides that a patient in a state hospital—certified as being 'mentally ill' and who has previously committed a crime—may be transferred without any hearing to a hospital for the criminally insane. A business recently was abolished by a Board of Health through an amendment of its rules that was made without notice or opportunity to be heard even by the business in question."

Obviously Justice Douglas would like to see all of the guarantees of the present Bill of Rights—and additional provisions, designed for modern problems—applied to all state legislation and state actions as well as to all federal proceedings.

"The advantage of private enterprise over socialism is the manner in which it releases the energies, the imaginations, and the inventiveness of men," Justice

164

Douglas said in this address. "The advantage of fair procedures when the lone individual challenges those in power is that government becomes the symbol of justice, not the badge of oppression."

The Supreme Court in modern times has been striving to see to it that state government, as well as federal government, is a symbol of justice for all—for poor persons without highly paid lawyers, for colored persons as well as white persons, for Americans of all kinds living in towns and cities or on the farms. To the Court, in this era, Americans are not primarily considered as residents of New York or North Carolina, of California or Texas, but as citizens of one nation.

Professor Robert G. McCloskey, in his excellent book entitled *The American Supreme Court,* has pointed out: "The Court has always tended to focus on the great open questions that plagued America as a whole—the nation-state problem from 1789 to 1860, the business-government problem from 1865 to 1937. . . . Within the limits of what it regards as its capacities, the Court can be expected to preoccupy itself with the issues that most preoccupy America. And civil rights is just such an issue. . . . In turning its attention to this subject, the Court was acting in perfect historical character." Mr. McCloskey added: "The Supreme Court, being an American institution, is obliged always to reckon with America and her propensities; and America is a nation that moves hesitantly and changes

165

gradually. In spite of our occasional frenzies, the great alterations in the Republic's development have been the result of long experience and slowly growing conviction. There are those on the modern Court—Justice Black and Douglas are the leading exemplars—who would resolve constitutional uncertainties with large, bold, pioneering strokes of the pen. If this is the proper model for judicial governance, then history is indeed an untrustworthy guide."

The question before this generation may be whether history can any longer be considered as a guide, trustworthy or untrustworthy. With astronauts orbiting the planet in a few minutes of flight, with communications satellites bringing pictures and words from Arabia to America almost instantaneously, with the newly emerging nations of Africa and Asia seeking to make giant strides in a few years, there are many signs that this is the most revolutionary age in which human beings have ever lived.

Biologists are looking into the very structure of life. Psychologists are developing new theories of human personality. Physicists are able to explore the inner core of matter. Astronomers anticipate new telescopes, located in space, that will bring us more knowledge of the universe than we have ever dreamed of having in past decades.

If America is to survive, perhaps America will have to change with greater intelligence and greater speed than America has ever shown before. If America is to be a leader in the newly developing community of man, perhaps the states will have to give up many of their old powers.

After all, the states were established to serve their people, just as the federal union was. If the people want the Bill of Rights applied everywhere, the state governments will finally accept the will of the people.

If automation largely eliminates work in the coming decades, it is clear that state authorities will not be able to cope with the problem of providing education and opportunities for creative activities to the many millions of Americans who will be seeking such education and such opportunities.

If the nations move toward a "world political community"—as Pope John XXIII has urged the nations to do, and as other leaders have predicted—new definitions of the Rights of Man will have to be developed, discussed, and extended to all human beings.

The problem of applying the American Bill of Rights to the people of all the states in the federal union of the United States may gradually become the problem of applying a Bill of Rights to all the people of the world. America may then be one state in a federal union of nations.

XIII Could We Lose the Bill of Rights?

THE STORY of America's development as a constitutional democracy is one of the great stories in history. It has been described from many aspects. It has been studied from many angles by Europeans, Asians and Africans as well as Americans. It is not fully understood—and it will never be completely comprehended because it involves the tremendous mystery of how people learn to govern themselves.

169

All historians agree that one vital factor in keeping America free is the preservation of the Bill of Rights. According to surveys, most Americans believe in the Bill of Rights, yet relatively few know what it contains or what would happen to them if it should be lost. Few of us relate the Bill of Rights to our personal lives—and yet every one of us, young and old, depends upon those rights for our freedom to speak without fear, our opportunity to belong to the church of our choice, our liberty to work where we please and to vote for any leaders we choose to represent us.

Under the Constitution originally adopted by our Founding Fathers, we had no specific charter of liberties. It wasn't necessary to spell out the rights of Americans, Alexander Hamilton said. As long as the love of liberty flourished in American hearts, no tyrants could enslave us. Other leaders who wrote the Constitution agreed with Hamilton.

As we have noted earlier, it took strenuous efforts by Thomas Jefferson and James Madison to get the Bill of Rights adopted. It has taken strenuous efforts and strong devotion by many Americans to keep the principles of the Bill of Rights alive in times of war and uneasy peace. In the present age of social, economic, and scientific revolutions, the meaning of the Bill of Rights requires new thinking and new dedication.

Much depends upon the knowledge and the attitudes of the young people of America. There are indications that many young people do not have an ardent love of liberty in their hearts.

Polls taken not long ago on five college campuses in Southern California, covering 1,100 students, revealed that many of them were hazy about the Bill of Rights. Many were willing to limit the individual freedoms of their fellow citizens in various ways. They did not seem to realize that their own freedoms might disappear if our constitutional protections were weakened.

Nearly half of these students approved of "double jeopardy"—that is, the trying of a person twice for a serious crime; yet the Bill of Rights provides that a person once acquitted in such a case cannot be tried again for that offense.

About 49 percent said they would support the internment of "suspicious persons" in government camps in the event of a national emergency, and were vague about how they would attempt to decide whether persons were "suspicious" or not.

Nearly a third of them were willing to give the police authority to use wiretaps on private telephone conversations. (The Supreme Court has ruled that wiretapping is forbidden under federal law, and evidence obtained by wiretapping is not admitted in federal courts.)

Fifty-three percent of them would not allow a labor leader to invoke the protection of the Fifth Amendment in an investigation. (The Fifth Amendment in the Bill of Rights declares that no one can be compelled to testify against himself.)

Substantial support for censorship measures was expressed by these students. A third of them felt that a government investigating committee should have the power to question any newspaper editor who criticized the committee's work. About a fifth of them believed that the Postmaster General should have the power to ban books which he considered immoral or obscene.

In general, the attitudes of these students indicated that many young Americans regard the views of the community or the desires of government officials as paramount above the ideas of individual persons. Other surveys have indicated that American young people are confused about the Bill of Rights or do not see why the protections and guarantees stipulated in the Bill are needed in the twentieth century.

Former President Dwight D. Eisenhower, Chief Justice Earl Warren, and other leaders have expressed alarm over the erosion of American liberties. Through indifference and ignorance, our fundamental rights might be lost.

In an address at Defiance College, Ohio, in May of 1963, General Eisenhower urged Americans to renew their devotion to self-reliance, independence of spirit, and love of liberty. He said that the framers of our Constitution could not know that "in less than two centuries the immensity of domestic and international affairs would tend to create in us a feeling of individual helplessness. . . ."

Eisenhower declared that some citizens had given way to "an unthinking abandonment of personal and local responsibility to a few men in government, giving to them a frightening power for good or evil—and almost certain to invite error or abuse."

In the same month, President Robert F. Goheen of Princeton University denounced the students who participated actively in a riot which damaged homes and other property there. In a letter to Princeton's undergraduates, Dr. Goheen said: "The collective surrender of selfhood by otherwise responsible individuals, and the inconvenience, danger and damage it worked against others, seem to me equally deplorable. . . . Its sheer wantonness and irresponsibility stood, of course, in particularly sharp juxtaposition to the deeply somber struggles [of the Negroes] in Birmingham."

Dr. Goheen said he was not disposed to take a gloomy view of the new college generation in America. He declared: "The unhappy madness of the night of May 6 has not changed my conviction that most of you will make fully as worthy contributions in the future as has any preceding generation of Princetonians. This letter, then, has not been written in despair. It is offered in the hope that we can all profit from searching and responsible reflection over issues of this sort."

Chief Justice Earl Warren chided the lawyers of the

nation for their failure to debate the issues presented by three proposed amendments to the Constitution. One amendment would permit state legislatures to amend the Constitution themselves without concurrence of Congress; one would create a Court of the Union, composed of the chief justices of each state, with power to review and override decisions by the U. S. Supreme Court; and a third amendment would deny federal courts the power to rule on the apportionment of seats in state legislatures.

"If proposals of this magnitude had been made in the early days of the Republic, the great debate would be resounding in every legislative hall and in every place where lawyers, scholars, and statesmen gather," the Chief Justice said. If the amendments were adopted, he felt that "the United States as we know it would be at an end."

He expressed astonishment and dismay at the fact that so little attention had been given to the dangers in these amendments. Supported quietly by a hard-core group of believers in state sovereignty, the amendments had been approved by legislatures in a number of states. Twelve states had approved the proposal to change the method of amending the Constitution; eleven had gone on record in favor of the Court of the Union, and four had approved the proposal to take away the federal power to determine the apportionment of seats in legislatures.

COULD WE LOSE THE BILL OF RIGHTS?

Governor George Romney of Michigan, a proponent for strong state governments, attacked the proposed amendments in an address at the National Press Club in Washington. The amendments went much too far, Romney felt. If adopted, the proposals would change our federal union into a weak confederation of the kind which had proved to be unworkable in the early days of the nation.

"Mutilation of the federal government will not strengthen the states," Governor Romney declared.

How could such amendments get approval by state legislatures without a thorough public discussion? How far has an attitude of irresponsibility sunk into the fiber of the American character? How many of us have fallen into the condition that General Eisenhower called "an unthinking abandonment of personal and local responsibility"?

Some signs indicate that millions of Americans have done so. The loss of our fundamental liberties has become a real possibility.

If we lost our Bill of Rights, what would happen to our way of life?

Here are some of the things that could happen:

The government could keep young men in the military services for indefinite periods, without giving any explanation or justification for this policy.

Young men and women leaving school could be

assigned to jobs in industries where the government asserted that workers were needed. Young people could be forced to take these jobs.

Students protesting against government policies—including those who recently picketed the White House—could be thrown into federal prisons by order of the President.

Americans, young or old, could be required to give up their property for public use without compensation if local, state or federal authorities decided that such property was needed for public projects.

The books available for reading in American homes could be censored by the Postmaster General or local committees under city, state or federal ordinances. Since the First Amendment protections for free speech would be gone, there would be no legal grounds for objecting to the censorship.

The names of persons writing critical letters to their Congressmen might be turned over to the police, and such persons could be arrested and imprisoned for "bringing disrepute upon the federal government or federal officers."

Editors who printed articles in their newspapers criticizing the government would be subject to arrest at any time, night or day.

The programs of television and radio broadcasting

stations would be governed by rules dictated by the federal agencies regulating the stations.

If appeals were made to the courts, the judges would not be able to use the precedents established since the foundation of the United States—because these precedents, in civil liberties cases, are largely built upon the Bill of Rights.

The very quality of American life would be gone.

The independence, the willingness to speak out, which mark the true American everywhere, would be crushed.

The eager exuberance, the lively restlessness, of Americans—noted by all foreign observers, cited by many as evidences of the creative atmosphere in America—would give way to cringing manners, fear of the police, fear of informers, fear of freedom itself.

Could we lose our Bill of Rights?

Could we come to a day in America when a military patrol could come to the White House and take the President away?

Could we come to a day when military chiefs could declare elections null and void—as they have done in many countries?

Could these things happen here?

The answer rests in the minds and hearts of the rising generation of Americans. Certainly this generation

—and the generations before us—have tried to hold on to the basic freedoms written into our Constitution more than 175 years ago. Let us hope that this generation cares enough about these liberties to understand them, to defend them, and to see their priceless value.

XIV How We Can Keep Our Liberties

A<small>T THE</small> beginning of this book, we described how our rights were won—the long suffering of millions of human beings, the gradual development of the idea of man's dignity, and the bloody battles fought to gain certain freedoms for all people, white or colored, rich or poor, Christians or non-Christians, respectable citizens or persons in trouble with the law, solid taxpayers or wandering eccentrics.

Many men and women have demonstrated that they are willing to die for the cause of liberty. Others have regarded liberty as a myth—a dream without material existence or practical value. Some persons in our generation have given up their belief in the possibilities of democracy in a technical age and now believe that the problems of government are so complicated that they must be left to the experts.

If we are to keep our liberties, we must have a new birth of brotherly love. We must see the vision already clearly seen by the Reverend Martin Luther King, the Negro minister who went among the colored people of Birmingham while the flames and smoke of bombings were still in the air, and said to the people: "Violence is wrong." He overcame the spirit of hate with his own spirit of love.

For most of us, it is hard to love a person with a different accent, a different kind of face, a different religion, a different color, or a different view of life. There is a voice that speaks loudly within us, saying: "Why can't other people be like *us?* Why do we have to try to understand *them?* Why don't they understand us?" And there is another idea, often spoken: "Love is nonsense. People simply need to respect one another. Those who want to love and be loved are sick. Persons who respect one another have dignity. Respect for human dignity will preserve the rights of man."

Yet love is a form of respect. Love is not necessarily blind. Love sees the defects of men and women, the wrong uses they make of their freedom, and love hopes that they will learn to do better. Lasting love is not simply spontaneous affection; it acknowledges responsibilities and duties.

If we are to keep our liberties, we must have a big idea of what human beings are. Robert M. Hutchins, the great American educator, said once: "Nature will not forgive those who fail to fulfill the law of their being. The law of human beings is wisdom and goodness, not unlimited acquisition."

If we are to stay free we must resist the temptation to think of man as a collection of electrons and protons, as a material object like a house or an automobile. A man or woman is a mysterious being, with invisible dimensions.

How do we develop wisdom and goodness, the indispensable elements in a free society? Religious leaders say there is an unknown force in the universe, a force called grace, which leaps like lightning into a man's very being and changes him in a way that is beyond his understanding. And yet man must not merely count upon this grace, this gift of enlightenment, this sudden unseen rain.

To be free in today's world and in the world coming rapidly upon us, we must work and think. Perhaps we must change our notions of what thinking is. If all our ordinary work is done by machines, as it is likely to be in the near future, thinking must be a form of action for human beings.

Some philosophers have always contended that

181

thinking should be regarded as the highest form of action. The record of history shows that civilizations with great thinkers have been the civilizations with great achievements.

To develop wisdom and goodness, we must welcome the hunger to know and to grow now rising in the community of man. We have the joyful and painful privilege of realizing that ours is the first age in which all men can really claim the inalienable rights asserted in the American Declaration of Independence—the rights to life, liberty, and the pursuit of happiness.

In our age, all men and women can learn together and grow upward together, sharing in the torrent of information and knowledge poured upon us in the communications revolution. All of us can become like the astronauts, seeing the earth as a whole.

How many orbits are there to freedom and justice? Is the race into space a triumph for man or an escape for man from the problems he has not solved on earth? Where do we go from the stars? What do we live by?

These are the questions restless, revolutionary man faces in this age and the age to come. The swarming millions of human beings everywhere are filled with great expectations, seeking the abolition of war and an abundant life for all. A basic political philosophy, applicable to all, can be found in our Bill of Rights as interpreted by the Supreme Court in this century.

What is that political philosophy? It can be de-

182

scribed as a perpetual search for the utmost meanings of life, a search conducted with full freedom of the mind and of the spirit. In this philosophy, political institutions exist to make this search a continuing and unlimited endeavor.

Long ago Thomas Jefferson said: "Democracy is the only form of government that is not eternally at open or secret warfare with the rights of mankind." It is the responsibility of democratic nations in our time to foster a trend toward democracy throughout the world. Paradoxically, this trend can principally be fostered by the development of truer democratic institutions in the existing democracies.

The struggle in the world today between the forces of tyranny and the forces of freedom cuts across all national lines, all political parties, all divisions between East and West. It cannot be solved by war. It can only be ended by steady and intelligent application of the principles underlying our Bill of Rights and the Universal Declaration of Human Rights adopted some years ago by the United Nations.

Roger N. Baldwin, chairman of the board of directors of the International League for the Rights of Man, stated in a report published in October of 1962: "If progress toward human rights is measured by freedom from foreign rule and the national independence of peoples, the past year has shown advances so great that the end of long-established colonialism by European powers is clearly in sight. If it is measured by the dictatorial or one-party character of governments hostile to human liberties, the past year shows a sharp decline. Not only the Communist dictatorships, controlling almost half of mankind, tolerate no organized opposition, but also the few remaining fascist and feudal states, the new one-party African states, and the military governments which have taken over power in Latin America, Asia and Africa.

"Human rights in terms of political freedom and individual liberties of speech, press and association seem reasonably secure among about one-third of mankind.

"But it is significant for the future that the principles of human rights as set forth in the Universal Declaration are generally accepted as goals even among those States which in practice deny them. At the United Nations the efforts to implement them go steadily if slowly forward in studies, reports, seminars, declarations and minor international treaties. No delegation would dare openly flout those principles, based on personal rights as obligations of governments. . . .

"Despite the discouragements of the cold war, the arms race and the confusions of the transition from colonial rule to independence of so many peoples, the prospects for greater liberties for more people are encouraging to those who rate high the equality of States

184

and creating world-wide consciousness of the equality of peoples."

By "States" in this context, Mr. Baldwin referred to what we would ordinarily call "nations." His hopeful view about the possibility of developing "greater liberties for more people" has been shared by many other leaders in the United States and other countries.

Pope John XXIII opened a Council of the Roman Catholic Church in 1962 with a glowing statement: "We feel we must disagree with those prophets of gloom who are always forecasting disaster, as though the end of the world was at hand. In the present order of things, Divine Providence is leading us to a new order of human relations. . . ."

Respect for the constructive powers of the human race rests upon love and faith—a faith rooted in reason but ranging beyond the limits of what reason can bring under analysis.

As we have seen, the idea of democracy is based upon the idea of man as a being who freely chooses to live under rules he both discovers and makes. He discovers the laws of his own being, but he recasts these laws from generation to generation through his powers as a free and independent person.

In a true democracy, man is not regarded as fully human except in the community he builds with other free beings. He is a physical creature, dependent to a large degree upon others for his very sustenance. Yet his greatest works are not physical structures. His greatest works are those he builds with love and wisdom—and he learns what love is by communicating freely with others of his kind; he grasps wisdom by accepting and giving, by living in a community and learning the dignity of the weakest person as well as the mightiest.

That is what the Bill of Rights is all about.

That is what needs to be discussed in schools, in adult education courses, in Lions Clubs and Rotary Clubs, in women's groups, in church societies—wherever free Americans gather.

In Texas—one of the great states of our federal union, a state as large as many nations—leaders have taken a long stride toward public understanding of these ideas.

Under the leadership of Judge Myron A. Love, Bishop John E. Hines of the Episcopal Diocese of Texas, and other fine citizens, a Texas Bill of Rights Foundation has been established to promote discussion and understanding of our great charter of liberties.

Let us hope that Bill of Rights Foundations will be formed in every state in the American union. Let us hope that the Center for the Study of Democratic Institutions will be able to establish branches in every state and in other nations. Let us encourage all people to work together to develop greater liberties for all.

Index

INDEX

INDEX

189

INDEX

THE AUTHOR

Frank Kelly is presently in charge of the Fund for the Republic's information program and is staff director for the Mass Media Department of the Fund's Center for the Study of Democratic Institutions. To name just a few of his past activities, he has been a Presidential speech writer, a professor at Boston University, a war correspondent, and a contributor to numerous publications. He is the author of several books including *An Edge of Light, The Fight for the White House,* and *Reporters Around the World* (a juvenile), and is co-author of *Your Newspaper,* and *Men Who Make Your World.* Mr. Kelly makes his home in Santa Barbara, California, with his wife and two sons.